Pietro DiDonato,
the Master Builder

Pietro DiDonato, the Master Builder

Matthew Diomede

Lewisburg
Bucknell University Press
London: Associated University Presses

© 1995 by Associated University Presses, Inc.

All rights reserved. Authorization to photocopy items for internal or personal use, or the internal or personal use of specific clients, is granted by the copyright owner, provided that a base fee of $10.00, plus eight cents per page per copy is paid directly to the Copyright Clearance Center, 222 Rosewood Drive, Danvers, Massachusetts 01923. [0-8387-5289-6 $10.00 + 8¢ pp, pc.]

Associated University Presses
440 Forsgate Drive
Cranbury, NJ 08512

Associated University Presses
25 Sicilian Avenue
London WC1A 2QH, England

Associated University Presses
P.O. Box 338, Port Credit
Mississauga, Ontario
Canada L5G 4L8

The paper used in this publication meets the requirements of the American National Standard for Permanence of Paper for Printed Library Materials Z39.48–1984.

Library of Congress Cataloging-in-Publication Data

Diomede, Matthew, 1940–
    Pietro DiDonato, the master builder / Matthew Diomede.
      p. cm.
    Includes bibliographical references (p.) and index.
    ISBN 0-8387-5289-6 (alk. paper)
    1. DiDonato, Pietro, 1911–92 —Criticism and interpretation.
2. Italian Americans in literature. I. Title.
PS3507.I137Z63 1995
813'.52--dc 20   94-38036
                                                                      CIP

PRINTED IN THE UNITED STATES OF AMERICA

Dedication

This work is dedicated to my whole Italian family, especially my mother, my father, my dear Aunt Lena, and all my aunts who taught me the "verities" of endurance, hope, and compassion. My two poems, "In Another Time," about my father, and "My Dear Aunt Lena" try to capture the appreciation of these virtues.

To my wife I owe my love.

To my Dad, who worked with steel as a steelworker, as did Pietro DiDonato with cement:

In Another Time

I know where I
learned to arch my back,
praying to the desk in front of me, while
I write this poem
between intervals of reading.
In our cold basement,
wearing a hat and coat,
with tools scattered about, my father,
without any formal
education, read into the hours of my childhood.
It was a persistent thing—something I think of now . . .
some altar, receiving two prayers from
two different places.

MATTHEW DIOMEDE

© *Christianity and Literature* 37, no. 1 (Fall 1987): 38. Reprinted with permission

To my dear Aunt Lena, whose compassion and hope most resembled those virtues in Pietro DiDonato's Annunziata:

My Dear Aunt Lena

I will come to your grave
in New York from Missouri,
kiss the earth that holds you,
and speak to you.
I will miss your smile and the way
your pale, purple hand clenched mine
as you barely mumbled.
Like the solid, heavy earth that lies
between our two states, I still feel your hand.
Earth is that separation which makes me touch you.

MATTHEW DIOMEDE

© *Christianity and Literature* 37, no. 1 (Fall 1987): 66. Reprinted with permission.

Contents

List of Abbreviations / 9
Acknowledgments / 11

1. Introduction / 15
2. A Literary Biography / 17
3. *The Immigrant Saint: The Life of Mother Cabrini* / 23
4. *The Penitent* / 31
5. "Christ in Plastic" / 41
6. *The Love of Annunziata* / 47
7. *This Woman* / 56
8. *Christ in Concrete* / 71
9. *Three Circles of Light* / 89
10. Conclusion / 97

Appendix A: Personal Interview, 14 August 1990 / 99
Appendix B: Personal Interview, 8 August 1991 / 125
Appendix C: A Descriptive Bibliography / 138
Notes / 148
Bibliography / 154
Index / 161

Abbreviations

Abbreviations of works frequently used in the text appear below. These abbreviations will occur within parenthetical reference form along with appropriate page number.

PRIMARY WORKS OF PIETRO DIDONATO

FICTION

CC	*Christ in Concrete.* Indianapolis: Bobbs-Merrill, 1939.
TG	"The Gospels." Unpublished.
TW	*This Woman.* New York: Ballantine, 1959.
TCOL	*Three Circles of Light.* New York: Julian Messner, 1960.

NONFICTION

CIP	"Christ in Plastic." *Penthouse,* December 1978, 3, 76, 78, 82, 222–24, 229–31.
IS	*The Immigrant Saint: The Life of Mother Cabrini.* New York: McGraw-Hill, 1960.
TP	*The Penitent.* New York: Hawthorn, 1962.

DRAMA

LOA	*The Love of Annunziata.* In *American Scenes,* edited by William Kozlenko, 119–38. New York: McGraw-Hill, 1991.

Interviews of Pietro DiDonato by the Author

DIOM Diomede, Matthew. "A Personal Interview with Pietro DiDonato, Held 14 August, 1990." "A Personal Interview with Pietro DiDonato, Held 8 August 1991." "A Descriptive Bibliography of Pietro DiDonato." In "Pietro DiDonato, The Master Builder: Constructing a Better World with Concrete and Love. A Study of Selected Works and of the Author." Ph.D. diss., St. Louis University, 1992. Page references are to the Appendixes in this volume.

Acknowledgments

I want to thank the inspiring teachers I had at Saint Louis University: Dr. Al Montesi, Dr. Ray Benoit, Dr. Helen I. Mandeville, and Fr. Walter J. Ong, S.J.

To Dr. Ronald DiLorenzo, Dr. Clarence Miller, Dr. Vince Casaregola, and Dr. Thomas R. Knipp, I offer gratitude for their encouragement and guidance. To Dr. Melvin Backman of Long Island University, C. W. Post Center, I show my appreciation for teaching me to look beyond the surface of things.

I also thank other professors at Long Island University: Professors Phyllis Dircks, Jeanne Welcher, Richard Griffith, Dan Levin, Martin Greenberg, Ivonne Rodax, and David Petteys.

To Dr. Sally M. Gall of New York University, I show my appreciation.

I want to also acknowledge the patience and typing abilities of my dedicated typist, Clare Mulch.

I cannot here mention so many others who have helped me.

To Mom I also offer my appreciation.

Finally, I acknowledge Pietro DiDonato, my Italian-American Paesano, who displayed to me in person and in his work the same virtues my very own Italian family displayed: generosity, warmth, compassion, genuine interest, and love. I acknowledge his spirit, as well as my Mom's and Dad's spirits in the following previously unpublished poem:

A Prayer to the Dead—To Mom and Dad—
St. Louis, Missouri

Written after Reading Pietro DiDonato's
Christ in Concrete, Published in 1939

We live in an
imperfect world where
the living defame the dead—
some wildflower sustaining
itself in summer heat
only to drop its seed
for winter's burial—
only the dead are perfect.
This is why I shall not forget
my mother or father.

MATTHEW DIOMEDE

Pietro DiDonato, the Master Builder

1
Introduction

The purpose of this study is twofold. First is the effort to make better known the artistic stature of Pietro DiDonato and to provide some basis for a deeper understanding of his work. Second is to achieve, through an exploration of his seven works, an insight into the creative process that he employs. While reviewing this critical material surrounding the DiDonato corpus, I immediately perceived that there was too little research done around his work. Critics such as Barbara Bauer have maintained that DiDonato's works and those of two other Italian writers "have gone relatively unnoticed in the annals of American literary scholarship,"[1] while Michael Esposito asserts that "both it *[Christ in Concrete]* and the rest of his [DiDonato's] fiction have attracted little attention,"[2] especially "outside the sphere of ethnic and American immigrant literature."[3] Giovanni Sinicropi believes that the bibliography on DiDonato and *Christ in Concrete* is "almost nonexistent,"[4] and he mentions that Rose Basile Green's book, *The Italian-American Novel*, does not list "one single item of critical bibliography on DiDonato."[5] Moreover, there is no single whole-book study of the work at all. A need therefore exists.

On 14 August 1990, I met with DiDonato in a face-to-face interview. During the discussion he kept referring to certain ideas and beliefs that were prevalent in his works. Using these ideas and beliefs as a reference frame, I have traced them in my analysis of seven of DiDonato's works; that is, as they recur in two biographies, one drama, an essay, and three novels. In Appendix A and B, I also include two personal interviews, held at his home, one on 14 August 1990, and another on 8 August 1991. In chapter 2, I link concepts about dreams and the taking on of male and female components,[6] since these play a part in understanding DiDonato and his works. Chapter 2, therefore, presents a conceptual framework for DiDonato's work that I discuss. Appendix C is a presentation of a descriptive bibliography of DiDonato's work, especially the seven works I cover in chapters 3 to 9. This chapter was modeled on

Edith Heal's book on William Carlos Williams, *I Wanted to Write a Poem*. In a similar manner, I asked Pietro DiDonato to talk of these seven works on August 1991, and to talk of the creation of them, and to add anything he thought might prove helpful to someone analyzing his works. With Thomas Carlyle's statement in mind that writing is a most miraculous thing, I feel I captured something about DiDonato's creative process of writing, and I discovered the "concrete" connections between the man and his works.

2

A Literary Biography

Pietro DiDonato, Italian-American bricklayer-writer, son of parents from Abruzzi, Italy, was born in Hoboken, New Jersey, in 1911. Some of his works tell stories of a journey, a quest to become a person, primarily through an autobiographical Paul or Paulo. At twelve, Paul, like Pietro, lost his father when his father, a construction worker, fell from a work scaffold. Paul, like Pietro, assumed the role of father in raising and supporting his mother and seven sisters. These autobiographical elements in three novels and a play also recount the journeys of other people, especially those of Paul's mother and father, which are central to an understanding of Paul's journey. Carl G. Jung believed that all dreams could be valuable if interpreted correctly.[1] All future references to DiDonato's works and my work will be abbreviated as listed earlier. Paul's dream/nightmare in *Christ in Concrete* (*CC*, 292–98) is vital to understanding the whole corpus of DiDonato's literature, especially his longer fiction and his play. In examining DiDonato's works in greater detail in chapters 3 to 9, the author has traced certain concepts, beliefs, and ideas expressed in various interviews with him (see chapter 2 and appendices A, B, and C of this work). Combining all these ideas and materials, the author presents an explanation of the man and his works.

The growth of Paul is central to the corpus of DiDonato. In the corpus, Paul, the Old Adam, becomes New Adam. By the term "New Adam" is meant a person who experiences a rebirth, a sense of liberation that occurs when one destroys what appears to destine him not to fulfill himself. This may be some "sin," some sense of doom that drives him to hate self, others, and life itself. But before Old Adam becomes New Adam, he must overcome his "original sin." The "original sin" of Paul follows and is caused by his father's death. In DiDonato's interviews with the author, he told him that to this day he still dreams of his father, and in those dreams he still lays bricks on jobs, and he is still falling off scaffolds, as his father did (*DIOM*, 102–3). Pietro claims,

"My father's death weighed on me..." (*DIOM*, 102). Moreover, central to Paul's dream/nightmare in *Christ in Concrete* (*CC*, 292–98) are two concepts: that Paul brings back "home" his father, Geremio, who has betrayed his wife, Annunziata, and that he does so "without hurting his feelings" (*CC*, 297). In this dream/nightmare, Paul yells to his father and the men on the job that they should "refuse to die" (*CC*, 297). Yet in this dream/nightmare, Paul appears to fall and die like his father. Paul's attempt to forgive his dead father (to not hurt him) was to be part of that journey of redemption of a New Adam, the new Paul. Paul's anger and his love of his mother were also to be part of his journey. Paul's refusal to die in his dream/nightmare in *Christ in Concrete* (*CC*, 297) is intricately connected to his taking on of a Father and a Mother, of male and female components.[2] In DiDonato's literature, I cover, most notably in *This Woman*, Paul's rejection of his father's statement, made to him in that dream/nightmare of *Christ in Concrete* (*CC*, 292–98): "Ah, not even the Death can free us, for we are ... Christ in concrete..." (*CC*, 298).

What is the "original sin" of Paul from which he must be freed? Paul believed his father's sin of adultery and his own sins of adultery were what would bring him to die, a belief which is epitomized in his statement in *Three Circles of Light*: "We had been punished by Heaven for Father's immorality, as religion constantly cried that the wages of sin was death" (*TCOL*, 245). In *Three Circles*, after his father's death, Paul learns "the sense of sin and the fear of God" (*TCOL*, 246)—the consequences of sin (*TCOL*, 246). In the same work, Paul becomes angry at the religiosity of his mother, who forgives "an erring father"[3] and who believes Paul's father is an "angel in heaven."[4] This anger at his mother and father is part of Paul's "original sin." In the early sections of *This Woman*, Paul feels impelled to repeat his father's sins of adultery (*TCOL*, 41; 86–87); Paul also drives his wife insane by not respecting and accepting her identity and her past *(TW)*.

Nevertheless, in *This Woman*, Paul finds himself, and he becomes a man, a New Adam, for he forgives his father's sins, accepts and forgives his father's past, accepts and forgives his wife and her past and finally accepts and forgives his own past and himself. Then Paul becomes head of a "home" filled with a love that his mother and sister would admire. Thus, a spiritually dead Paul (Old Adam) comes alive (New Adam) in *This Woman*, because he frees himself of his "original sin," his sense of doom. Thus, Paul becomes more compassionate and less egocentric in *This Woman*, again resembling his sister and mother who loved Geremio.

The corpus of DiDonato's works covered in this study traces Paul's development to his fullest growth in *This Woman*. Though Paul first crushes his mother's crucifix in *Christ in Concrete* (CC, 304–5), his mother forgives him, and he, likewise, forgives her (CC, 305–7, 309–11). In *Christ in Concrete*, however, Paul takes on a Mother, the female component, but he takes on a Father, a male component, *only* in his dream/nightmare in *Christ in Concrete* (CC, 292–98). It is not until *This Woman* that Paul can forgive and accept his Father, the male component. In the play *The Love of Annunziata*, Paul is more "neutral," in the sense that DiDonato's emphasis is upon the love of Annunziata and her forgiveness of a man who betrayed her. When Paul becomes free of the consequences of his own father's sin ["original sin"], he becomes more of a man. In this sense, *This Woman* represents the culmination of the growth of Paul. In that novel, Paul fulfills his mother's prediction in *Christ in Concrete* that he will become a father to his children, and he arrives at "the flower of womankind" (CC, 311). Paul takes on the compassion of his mother and loves his father as he becomes a father in *This Woman*. In the same work, Paul fulfills an important part of the dream/nightmare in *Christ in Concrete* (CC, 292–98): in a psychological sense, Paul brings "home" his father "without hurting his feelings" (CC, 297).

This conceptual framework has helped the author understand DiDonato's three novels and his play, as well as the other works discussed. The dream/nightmare in *Christ in Concrete* (CC, 292–98), especially its positive aspects, becomes reality for Paul in *This Woman*. Paul, therefore, does not die in the "concrete" of death; he, like a new Adam, saves himself by accepting his wife Isa and by becoming a loving father *(TW)*.

During my interviews with Pietro, on 14 August 1990 and 8 August 1991 (see this chapter and appendixes A and B), I isolated certain of DiDonato's concepts, beliefs and ideas. These are traced in the works discussed in greater detail in chapters 3 to 9. In our discussion, DiDonato made the following points over and over again (see appendixes A and B in this book).

1. Love can shame death. (*DIOM*, 105)
2. Life takes place in mystery and that mystery contains the sacredness which results in love. (*DIOM*, 104–5, 113–14)
3. Dreams are valuable; you can't disregard them. They make "terrible" sense. (*DIOM*, 102–3)
4. I [DiDonato] am a protester with a sense of rebellion. (*DIOM*, 101)

5. The only God I have now is beauty and my wife. (*DIOM*, 100) "Love is God and woman is love." (*DIOM*, 143)
6. I [DiDonato] write a "story" with a "message." (*DIOM*, 104)

DiDonato's statement that love can shame death (*DIOM*, 105) means that in his corpus of literature one can overcome those obstacles in life that hinder him from becoming a better person. These obstacles are guilt, evil, hate, anger, jealousy, bigotry, the inequities of justice and the lack of finances. In *Immigrant Saint*, Saint Cabrini manages to help others despite numerous obstacles; in *The Penitent*, Alessandro Serenelli, murderer of Goretti, turns to love instead of hate with the help and love of Saint Maria Goretti and her family; she forgave him while he was killing her! The Italian-American sense of community and perseverance in *Christ in Concrete* provides renewal of life to all. Paul's sense of love for his mother and father is traced in all the novels and the play; its development ranges from anger and hate, especially in *Three Circles*, to a resolution culminating in love in *This Woman*. In DiDonato's essay, "Christ in Plastic," we arrive at an understanding of DiDonato's concept in a different manner, a reversal or negative sense, for Moro, Italy's President of the Christian Democrat Party, does not display love for the people he rules. Death, the opposite of love, controls his life and, ultimately, his destiny, in the form of an assassination.

Another of DiDonato's beliefs, that life takes place in mystery, which is not only sacred but is also love (*DIOM*, 104–5, 113–15), manifests itself in his works. As we study Paul in the novels and play, we see how he steadily undergoes a transformation for the better until he reaches the pinnacle in DiDonato's work, *This Woman*, which reflects the fulfillment of his mother's promise made in *Christ in Concrete* (*CC*, 311) that he would become Father by being a loving, compassionate person. So often the mystery of the dream world also deepens the works and life of DiDonato. To the author, DiDonato said that dreams (*DIOM*, 102) can make "terrible" sense. The dream/nightmare of Paul in *Christ in Concrete* (*CC*, 292–98) aids Paul in accepting his father's and mother's shortcomings in *This Woman*. He therefore accepts them totally and forgives them. In the other novels and one play this acceptance does not occur as fully for Paul as it does in *This Woman*. In another sense, *The Love of Annunziata*'s plot reveals a sense of mystery, a foreshadowing of the death of Geremio. On the other hand, Annunziata's mysterious dream of dancing the tarantella at Geremio's funeral indeed proclaims the mystery (power of forgiveness) and strength of her magnanimous love for a husband who betrayed her. The power of the dream world and mystery of life is also evident in *Immigrant Saint*, in which the author discusses how dreams and prayers helped Mother Cabrini solve her numerous problems and, in *The Penitent*, in which an important dream of Serenelli's changes the course of his life for the better.

DiDonato also told this author that the only God he has now is beauty and his wife (*DIOM*, 100). He also said, "Love is God and woman is love" (*DIOM*, 143). In his study of DiDonato's works, this author has used Jungian concepts of male (Father) and female (Mother) to demonstrate, as previously noted, the growth of Paul. In *This Woman*, Paul ultimately reflects the best of the feminine spirit (purity, compassion, truth, sincerity, honesty, hope, forgiveness), characterized by Annunziata, his sister Annina and even, eventually, his wife Isa. In addition, Paul will not be able to take on a Father, the male component, until he possesses those feminine qualities that Annunziata, Annina, and Isa represent. When Paul takes on these qualities, he is able to forgive and accept his father, thereby accepting him with courage and bravery, and eliminating the fear that is death (*TW*, 153; *TCOL*, 246). This acceptance takes time to develop. Paul most rejected his mother and father in *Three Circles*.

Not only does DiDonato define his God as beauty and his wife, but he also, more generally, loves all good and beautiful people (*DIOM*, 100–101, 105, 113–14), so it is little wonder he wrote two biographies relating to saints. Paul's repeated attempts to arrive at a love of his mother and father throughout DiDonato's corpus indicate a striving toward the good and beautiful. In addition, until Paul loves himself, he cannot love his wife or life itself. As the reader will see, the concept of love is related to Paul's acquisition of the feminine and male components. Even when DiDonato writes of the injustice of the Italian leader, Aldo Moro, in "Christ in Plastic," and even when he speaks of the cruelties of the treatment of the immigrants in *Christ in Concrete*, he speaks of "woman." For any system or person, especially a leader, without compassion, sensitivity or love, the lack of the feminine qualities represents a form of death which may perpetuate injustices on self and others, quite the contrary of what DiDonato would term "beauty," "woman," or "love."

When DiDonato called himself a protester with a sense of rebellion (*DIOM*, 101) and said he wrote by telling a "story" (*DIOM*, 104) with his "message" of the mystery of love and women, he was speaking of his entire oeuvre. All that he writes reflects these concepts. Applied in their most literal sense, when he wrote "Christ in Plastic," for instance, he was opposing the injustices of a government and its leader, Aldo

Moro. In its broadest sense, the continuity of plots and themes of the three novels and plays discussed in this work demonstrates the growth of an earlier, innocent, rebellious young boy Paul who passes into mature adulthood. These works trace the development of Paul, who protests his father's sin, his mother's innocence, his wife's identity, his mother's and sister's religiosity, the injustice of any unfair political, social, economic or religious system. Paul is most defiant in *Three Circles*, but he resolves this hate and anger in *This Woman*, where he finds "home" as a father after a bittersweet journey. Paul also brings his father "home ... without hurting his feelings" (CC, 297) and therefore fulfills the most positive aspirations of his dream/nightmare in *Christ in Concrete* (292–98), even though the betrayal of Annunziata by Geremio is mentioned often in all the novels and the play. Yet this author believes that the tremendous love Annunziata had for her husband (the feminine component) becomes an integral part of Paul in *This Woman*, in which he ultimately appears not to be in rebellion any longer. His role as a father brings him to reason. After he realizes he has driven his wife insane, he becomes a New Adam and casts off his guilt, anger and hate, the albatrosses of his life. This sin, the abuse of his wife, nearly drives him insane until he frees himself of that "original sin." This original sin is caused by his father's death. Paul, indeed, overcomes his sense of fear and the doom manifested in his father's sin and its consequences. At the end of *This Woman*, Paul, therefore, can now love. He is freed from death and the fear of death (*TW*, 253; *TCOL*, 246). His protest against father and mother has ended.

As will be shown, I trace the sensitive "story" and "message" of Paul's sense of rebellion to its resolution in the three novels and play. I believe the "concrete" which DiDonato creates is the "concrete" of love: what his Italian-American sense of community and the love of his parents manifested. In the final analysis, these autobiographical allusions represent love to DiDonato and, like brick work, the building of love is difficult and takes great effort. Paul, in *This Woman*, shows us that love can emanate from agony and pain. Yes, we, like a New Adam, can be saved.

3

The Immigrant Saint: The Life of Mother Cabrini

When Pietro DiDonato was asked to gather biographical material for a movie about St. Mother Francesca Xavier Cabrini, the idea never materialized; nevertheless, he used the materials to write a book, *The Immigrant Saint: The Life of Mother Cabrini* (*DIOM*, 139, 140).[1] The book was chosen as a main selection by the Catholic Book Club for January 1961, and by the Maryknoll Book Club for February 1961.[2]

When Pietro DiDonato provided the author an article by D. W. MacKinnon on creativity from *The Saturday Review*,[3] I could understand Pietro's appreciation of creativity in others and how that creativity was reflected in his own writing, especially his book on St. Mother Cabrini. He tells us about how Cabrini's own father, Agostino, was the exemplification of creative goodness and about how this creative love influenced Mother Cabrini early in life. In speaking of the problems of Italy's unification of the late 1800s, her father said that the governments of Austria and Italy acted as "cruel traps" (*IS*, 16), for they lacked the "love of Christ" (*IS*, 16). He also stated that "they cannot create, they destroy" (*IS*, 16). DiDonato has done a careful job of showing how Agostino's daughter, St. Cabrini, spent her life following her father's words about creating rather than destroying. DiDonato's book points out that Francesca Cabrini was a symbol of endurance, patience, courage and love as she worked for others in establishing orphanages, hospitals, convents, and visiting prisons. Her actions and words were exemplifications of her dreams and her prayers. It is the author's intent to highlight the dreams and some of her beautiful prayers that were to make Francesca a saint. As DiDonato says of Mother Cabrini, "A dream, an instinct" often "suggested her decision" (*IS*, 159). In one interview, DiDonato also indicated that dreams are vital throughout his works (*DIOM*, 102–3, 113–14). Moreover, according to Carl G. Jung, every dream, if interpreted correctly, can help a person grow.[4]

Throughout St. Cabrini's biography, DiDonato shows us how her beautiful dreams contribute to her creative life of prayer and action. Francesca, herself, tells us how dreams helped her solve her problems as she went to her room "and [would] sleep like a baby, for when I lay my head on the pillow, Jesus, my Spouse, comes and takes from me to solve for me during the night, the cares of our Missionary Sisters" (*IS*, 116). DiDonato early in *Immigrant Saint* foreshadows the role that dreams will play in Francesca's life when he contrasts her dreams to those of other children:

> Her dreams were different from those of other children and more fervent. Her schoolmates dreamed of heroes and heroines of fabled lore, of Cinderella and fairy godmothers, of sorcerers and werewolves, of elves and ogres and crusading armies with knights and knaves. Francesca knew these tales, but one by one, beside the great passion within her, they burst like bubbles. She had a wonderland of her own, and dreamed of Him [God] who is the most true. (*IS*, 5–6)

Prefacing a catalog of some of these delightful dreams that seem to prompt her to some prayerlike action, especially when insoluble problems present themselves, two comments should be made: Mother Cabrini solves problems as one would slay dragons (see note 4 to chapter 6); and, as DiDonato says so well, Francesca has a way of converting agony into love: "Tragedy, which terrorizes and crushes the spiritually blind, ennobled her" (*IS*, 21). Francesca's whole life is the epitome of DiDonato's own statement in an interview, that love can shame death (*DIOM*, 105). His other statement, that life is a "mystery" and is also "sacred," is relevant to her life (*DIOM*, 104–5, 113–14).

Cabrini's first dream relates to her desire to be a missionary. From childhood she had this desire, and one day she almost died as a child in acting out her dream. She cut flowers in her uncle Don Luigi's garden by a river and placed them in little paper boats she made with scissors, and dispatched the boats to China (*IS*, 7–8):

> "Sister Daisy and Sister Geranium and Sister Violet, I am sending you across the ocean to far away China to save souls for our Lord. Do not be afraid. Be brave and do not cry. I, your mother, will pray for you, and you will be safe. God bless you, Sisters of the flowers." (*IS*, 8)

While leaning over an embankment, she fell over it and nearly drowned (*IS*, 8–9). Later in her life, at the House of Providence, an orphanage and convent that was finally dissolved by Bishop Gelmini because of improprieties, misuse of funds, abuse of children (not due to her but primarily because of the faults of a vivacious nun, Sister Antonia Tondini), Cabrini has a dream. This dream foreshadows the establishment of a new missionary convent, a visit to St. Peter's in Rome, and a request to travel west in missionary work (*IS*, 38–39):

> That was the first night in the House of Providence that she went to her bed with an unclouded Peace. . . .
>
> *It is the twilight of the new day. She knows not or questions whether her vision is dream or waking. He [God] is pointing to the Franciscan Church in Codogno, then to St. Peter's and the dovecotes within the cornices, then He directs His hand toward the West-reaching ocean.* Following morning prayer, she hastened to the Franciscan church which was in the quiet wooded section of town. There seemed to be nothing but trees behind the church. She persistently searched the vicinity, and in the woods discovered an ancient abandoned monastery . . . the Mission of the Sacred Heart! (*IS*, 38–39)

This phenomenon of being between the dream and waking stage is depicted as a source of creativity in Hawthorne's *The Scarlet Letter*.[5]

Another mystical event which appears to be unrelated to Cabrini's dreaming but may account for her mysterious ability to have these holy dreams is one in which another nun, in an adjoining bed is awakened (*IS*, 42), and actually visualizes a halo around Cabrini as Cabrini sleeps. "About Francesca Cabrini's short golden hair and face there was light. Her expression was of transfiguration, her eyes reflected a flaming vision" (*IS*, 42). Thereafter, "Cabrini would sleep in a little room by herself" (*IS*, 42).

An account of her several dreams seems appropriate here. Once the House of Providence was established at Codogno, Cabrini had a second dream telling her to go to Rome to expand her work (*IS*, 46). After initially being denied permission to do so by Monsignor Sellati (*IS*, 46), and after being denied permission by Cardinal Parocchi to establish a foreign mission and a mother house at St. Peter's, because "her institute was too small, its background brief, and it has no money" (*IS*, 51), she succeeds, nevertheless, at fulfilling all these goals (*IS*, 52). Her unwavering confidence in God above all was evident in her holy words, "Neither men, circumstances, nor devils can stop me!" (*IS*, 53). DiDonato tells of another dream that led to her success: "Christ appeared to her as a child and said, 'Francesca, go to that ground where they crucified Peter. Go to the rock where flames the light eternal. Francesca, Rome is thy portal'" (*IS*, 46). In time, her dream was actualized. Her visit to Rome was successful. Her childhood dream of sending nuns around the world in boats was, indeed, to have its real beginning with this second dream.

Her third sequence of dreams dealt with the vision, when she was thirty-eight, of serving as missionary. As a child, she had always wanted to serve in the Orient (*IS*, 8). When she was told by Vatican Bishop Scalabrini that she was needed in New York by Archbishop Corrigan to care especially for Italian orphans (*IS*, 57, 59), she seemed to lose courage. However, before she was to appear before the Pope, she had a dream/vision. Her mother appeared to her. Again, DiDonato aptly describes her dream/vision:

> She was on the bank of the swift-moving Venera River placing flowers as her nuns in a large paper boat to waft across the ocean, but she feared to get into the boat herself. Her mother appeared and said emphatically, "Francesca mine, and what is it? Afraid? Daughter, courage is wanting! Why did you say, 'I am going to become a missionary?' Did you mean it, or were you pretending? And now why are you reluctant to leave the Christian soil of your people?" Then in silent procession appeared Saint Catherine, Saint Teresa, Saint Francis Xavier and beautiful Virgin Mary. Finally, her Spouse came to her, and about His glowing Sacred heart and impressed upon His white robe was His name, enwreathed with red roses. "My child and bride, what fear thee? Knowest thou not that prayer bringeth passion, and My love in return bringeth strength? I send thee to bear My name in a distant land. Then, be courageous and fear not, for I am ever with thee, and with Me thou canst do all things." (*IS*, 58–59)

When Mother Cabrini told Bishop Scalabrini about this dream, he joked about her dreams and then opened a letter stating that she must go to New York (*IS*, 59).

Mother Cabrini's fourth prophetic dream concerned moving the location of her New York orphanage to another location, West Park, situated on the Hudson River. First, previous to her dream, Archbishop Corrigan felt the orphanage in the city was "badly located" (*IS*, 84). "Politicians, real estate men and the complacent rich resented an orphanage" (*IS*, 84) in that part of the city. Francesca herself desired an orphanage in a rural setting much like her father's farm in San Angelo, Italy. To the Archbishop she described her dream in detail (*IS*, 85). Then he took her to a place in Peekskill, but instead she looked to the opposite shore (*IS*, 85) and she said, "Ah, Excellence, . . . there, that is the place where our orphans should be" (*IS*, 85). The 450 acres belonged to the Jesuits (*IS*, 87). She said, "This is the very place I saw in my dream" (*IS*, 87). She also made another prediction about this place, which was to come to pass at the end of her life. "Here, will I be buried on the gentle slope overlooking the river" (*IS*, 88).

Closely related to the fourth dream is the next problem, that, though willing to sell the property, the Jesuits could not discover water on it, even after using the services of several well drillers (*IS*, 88). Water would have to be hauled from the river far below (*IS*, 88). Cabrini's gallant response to the Jesuits who were concerned about her caring for orphans indicates her strong faith in Providence: "Dear Brothers, remove that concern [for the children] from your conscience and let it rest upon my shoulders. If our Lord wants me to raise His children here in West Park, he will bring water" (*IS*, 88). In addition, though she had not a penny in the bank to buy this property, she told a sister nun and the Jesuits, "Our Lord is my banker and will not fail to help me find the money. These problems overcome my naturally weak condition and make me strong! The bigger the problem, the stronger I become" (*IS*, 88). She eventually found benefactors who helped her, but the water problem still existed. Then she had a dream where she prayed to Our Lady, and Our Lady appeared, indicating where the well should be dug (*IS*, 90). After the dream, she led a well driller to the spot, where they discovered water (*IS*, 90). At this point of discovery she placed a statue of the Blessed Virgin (*IS*, 90).

The sixth dream of Mother Cabrini had to do with her pursuing and continuing her hospital mission, since she was extremely sensitive to the sight of pain and "nauseated by hospital smells" (*IS*, 109), and she wondered if she could put up with the labor involved. She was also affected by a particular incident. A sick Italian at the East 109 Street Hospital in New York could not read a letter that he thought was from his mother in Italy (*IS*, 109). A sister read the letter, notifying him of his mother's death (*IS*, 90). When Francesca heard the story, she wept (*IS*, 109). As a result, she became despondent about hospital work, especially since the hospital had additional problems concerning management and finances (*IS*, 90, 108). DiDonato carefully describes how a dream again gave Cabrini her direction and courage to continue her work when the Virgin Mary appeared in that dream:

> A dream relieved her of her repugnance [for hospital work]. In the dream she was in a hospital and beheld a most beautiful and delicate lady who, with sleeves uprolled, was cheerfully changing the repulsive

bed sheets and tenderly cleansing the ghastly wounds of patients. Recognizing the Lady as the Virgin Mary, she [Francesca] rushed to help her. But the Mother of Christ smilingly waved her away, and softly said, "Francesca Cabrini, I will do this urgent work for you!" (*IS*, 109)

This remark from the Virgin Mary spurred Francesca to continue her work: "Madonna, whatever is worthy of Thy hands, I shall not deem beneath my efforts" (*IS*, 110). Because of problems at the 109 Street Hospital, Francesca then courageously moved her hospital to Twelfth Street, where she faithfully continued her work, uttering the beautiful prayer, "With my Christ, I can do all good works!" (*IS*, 110).

Another dream she had about doing her work in England (*IS*, 138) was to become a reality, when she established a "large residence in the London suburb of Honor Oak" (*IS*, 207–8).

Another dream was to help Mother Cabrini in her effort to locate and build an orphanage in Seattle. The planned orphanage was in the "path of a planned city highway" (*IS*, 215). On foot, she sought other places for construction, but she could not find any suitable place. Finally she placed a map of Seattle before her daughter nuns, pointed to a location, and sent them there. One daughter, who knew Seattle, reaffirmed that no location could be found there. Nevertheless, the daughters left and returned to Mother Cabrini, telling her they had found a "little paradise on earth" (*IS*, 215). Mother Cabrini responded to them that she had visualized the exact place in a dream: "I knew it would be a beautiful place. I saw it all, in my dream" (*IS*, 215). Upon asking the proprietor about the possibility of buying the land, the proprietor told her that his wife, the owner of the estate, would not sell. Evening came, and while Francesca was in the village, a "chauffeur-driven limousine approached" (*IS*, 216). Mother Cabrini raised her cane and signaled (*IS*, 216). The car stopped and drove her back to the convent. In the limousine she told a rich woman of the property she wanted to buy. When they arrived at the convent, the lady desired a glass of water and requested to come into the convent. Cabrini complied to these wishes. When Cabrini was asked by Archbishop O'Dea how she was given the property by the woman, she replied, "Excellence, I paid for it with three treasures: my love, a dream, and a glass of water in His name" (*IS*, 216). (Strangely enough, this rich woman turned out to be the owner of the property!) This little story so much reminds me of DiDonato's own story in our interview (*DIOM*, 104–5) that life occurs in a mystery: no matter what we do, it takes place in mystery; love results from this sacredness. Love can shame death (*DIOM*, 113–14).

In the United States, with her creditors and benefactors abandoning her efforts to establish another Seattle foundling home, her dreams were again to assist her (*IS*, 225–26). When a Mr. Hilbery, president of the Scandinavian Bank, appeared at her residence, Francesca spoke to a sister nun of having seen him in a dream: "Daughter, you quickly and most respectfully, admit Mr. Hilbery. Last night, while I slept briefly, I had a dream of great good" (*IS*, 226). Shortly after his visit, she was granted a mortgage to purchase the Perry Hotel (*IS*, 226). This dream followed an episode in which Francesca had placed her written wishes on a book which was part of a statue of Saint Anna, the mother of Mary, reading to Mary (*IS*, 227).

Another dream was to help St. Cabrini change her idea about building the orphanage in the Perry Hotel in Seattle. She, instead, changed her mind and built what was to become the Seattle Columbus Hospital. Again, calling upon her benefactor, Saint Anna, to help her, Cabrini recounts the dream:

"Saint Anna, being destined as the patroness of the new house, the worries devolve upon her, and it is she who has to work. She herself will do all for the new house. . . . Last night, in a dream, she told me what to do. . . . 'The time is not propitious for your original intention here. Turn about your plan so that it walks on its own legs.' Thus Saint Anna instructed me to relinquish my desire of a foundling home and indicated instead a hospital that will do works of mercy and yet sustain itself." (*IS*, 227)

As DiDonato's biography shows, Mother Cabrini's sense of prayer was so firmly rooted in her life that one can understand how she overcame so many of her difficulties. Some of these, to name a few, were her frail condition (*IS*, 1, 14, 19, 22–24, 33, 147, 151, 193, 201, 210, 223, 234), her difficulties encountered on the job (*IS*, 53, 69, 72, 76, 80–82, 90, 110, 163), especially the crude treatment received from Sister Tondini in her first moments of being a nun (*IS*, 23–27, 32, 34, 37, 209). Cabrini's powerful prayers—many of them reported in the biography—helped her resolve her problems, though the biography contains so many other prayers I will not mention. Her life was a total dedication to God, despite all her troubles. She addressed a daughter nun with a lesson on faith: "Child, you have troubles? With fifty houses to think about, I have none. Let us abandon ourselves to God, oh, dear daughter mine; let us be conducted and guided by Him, let us do His Will, and then our faces will not be pallid, but always placid and radiant" (*IS*, 196).

Like her faith itself, Mother Cabrini's sense of time is permeated with a strong sense of love. Fr. William F. Lynch, S.J., in *Christ and Apollo,* once said that "it is not too much to say that in the attitude we take toward time, as the most intense form of the limited, or our decision either to strain against it or to accept it, depends our peace."[6] Cabrini's sense of time and of evil occurring within time involves a love of God: "We must return darkness with light, epithets with forgiveness and prayer. His gifts were not meant to be cast away by strife. Love is time, love is space, love is forever, and He is love" (*IS,* 32). Appreciating the sense of time in her life, she forgave that cruel Sister Antonia Tondini, who maltreated not only her but the orphans: "Antonia Tondini was given by God not to know any better. She truly thought, when she treated me the way she did, that it was for my good" (*IS,* 209).

In *Immigrant Saint,* DiDonato does a wonderful job of showing how Cabrini's dreams and prayers were vitally connected to her world of action. The love and sense of mystery[7] DiDonato talks about in his own experience of life (*DIOM,* 104–5) is evident in the biography of Mother Cabrini.

As the DiDonato interviews (Appendixes A, B, and C in this book) suggest, his views and those presented in his portrait of Mother Cabrini are very much alike. One must consider the possibility that DiDonato simply projected his intense belief in Catholicism and his views of love and the mystery of life onto the character that he draws of Cabrini. Is it possible that either is not genuinely smitten by love of the major figures of Catholic belief? The author believes not, but the final judgments must rest with the reader.

4
The Penitent

Carl Jung, in *Modern Man in Search of a Soul*, believes that every dream, if interpreted correctly, can have meaning. Questioned about this belief, Pietro DiDonato has acknowledged that dreams are valuable and are frequently used in his works (*DIOM*, 102–3). In DiDonato's *Immigrant Saint*, as has already been shown, dream was extremely important in St. Mother Cabrini's life. What the author wishes to do now is to trace the development of change for the better that occurred in Alessandro Serenelli, the murderer of St. Marietta (Maria) Goretti, about whom DiDonato wrote in his second biography, *The Penitent*. A vital dream of Alessandro accounts for part of this change, though other influences are also evident—one being the pervasive, forgiving spirit of the Goretti family, including the influence of Maria Goretti and her mother, Assunta. Other influences include Alessandro's habit of reading and the experiences that followed his release from prison. DiDonato's comments to the author about love shaming death (*DIOM*, 105) and life being strange and sacred (*DIOM*, 104–5, 113–15) certainly play a part in the biography of *The Penitent*, as demonstrated in Alessandro's and Maria's lives.

After completing *Immigrant Saint*, DiDonato tells about the genesis of *The Penitent*:

> [My] wife read of her and the attempted rape. She said Maria was a second St. Agnes. The Passionist Fathers postulated her cause. I knew these priests in West Hoboken, New Jersey. I went to church there, knew the priests, and the story was relevant to me. The Passionist Fathers gave me so much material, including a letter to the Pope. I wrote an outline, and got a contract from Prentice-Hall.[1]

The Penitent was then published in 1962; it was inspired by DiDonato's wife[2] and dedicated to her (*TP*, dedication page).

In this work, DiDonato is very skillful in describing the mind and emotions of a twenty-year-old man, Alessandro, who kills a twelve-year-old girl, Maria Goretti, when she resists an attempted rape. DiDonato's efforts in describing the thoughts and emotions of a murderer are similar to the efforts of two other writers: Robert Louis Stevenson in "Markheim" and Dostoyevsky in *Crime and Punishment*. Both the Serenelli and Goretti families were peasant migratory farm workers in Italy.

For five years Alessandro had been at sea, during which "life . . . was pagan" (*TP*, 13), and where the men enjoyed talking of "carnal sin" (*TP*, 13). Pietro, Alessandro's older brother, ordered him to help his father, working in the fields of Ferriere, Italy. Alessandro soon felt trapped on land (*TP*, 13, 184) and, like Markheim of Robert Louis Stevenson's story, Alessandro tried "to kill time" (*TP*, 184). Alessandro, however, tried "to kill time" through his reading, and this led him to some bad influences, stories of crime and violence:

> The isolated fret of the marshes would not spare me; it gave me no satisfaction and I sought to lose and appease myself in reading, as the saying goes, "just to kill time," but it seems, perhaps, that only death kills time.[3] It is to be admitted that the wrong kind of reading influenced my mind and conduct. . . . (*TP*, 184)

He read "popular" (*TP*, 17, 18) and "exciting" (*TP*, 17, 18) and sometimes questionable material. His young mind did not seem to operate in an ethical, logical fashion. After reading a work of Stendhal's, Alessandro believed, as Stendhal indicates in his work, that "the murderer had more soul in him than all the poets, and more wit than the gentlemen judging him!" (*TP*, 18). DiDonato also indicates several of Alessandro's underlined, notebook passages that were very much in the spirit of the crime he was to commit (*TP*, 19). Among the passages are some which are particularly relevant. Alessandro felt that the world was against him: "A peasant is a machine who opens the ground to put manure into it, till the day when he lies down in it to become manure himself" (*TP*, 19). His justification of his crime could be foreshadowed in the phrase, "To complete a truly great, a frenzied passion, a warm and ardent passion, a crime is a necessity" (*TP*, 19). His driving passion is also foreseen in the words, "Every man has in his heart a sleeping swine and the swine often awakens with horrible results. There is no brute so foul and cruel as to rival man in lubricity and cruelty. We are beasts that perish" (*TP*, 19).

4 / THE PENITENT

Alessandro tells us about another strong influence, the loss of his mother:

"The prime cause of my ruin was guideless upbringing without a mother. I told you [DiDonato] I never saw my mother. I heard my schoolteacher say, 'The greatest tragedy is the loss of a mother.'" (*TP*, 184)

Though too young to feel the influence of his mother, that influence would probably have been negative anyway. Alessandro's older brother, Pietro, saved Alessandro, "a mere baby" (*TP*, 15) when he was "thrown into the river by his deranged, tormented mother" (*TP*, 15). DiDonato also shows how the loss of the female component affected Alessandro's life negatively: "In his limited way he judged for himself that fate had conspired against him for him to be without mother and family" (*TP*, 16). Alessandro also explains the effect of not having a mother: "My mother died when I was a few years old. I never knew her. . . . No one can take the place of a mother. Without a mother's tender care and direction, my life started on a wrong foot" (*TP*, 179).

As DiDonato shows us how Alessandro's personality was shaped, he excellently describes the operation of Alessandro's mind at its most perverted stage: "He felt he had to prove something to himself; that he must seduce and conquer her [Maria Goretti's] strength because, to him, wrong seemed to be the only right. He must break a dread moral law, like a mute who shocks himself into speech" (*TP*, 23). This passage reminds one of Raskolnikov's thinking in *Crime and Punishment*. Alessandro's loss of control of the universe he lived in is evident in his thinking:

What appealed to him [Alessandro] and attracted him about Maria was the immolation of the pure, which meant to him a secret defiance of society, a perversion of goodness. That to him would be his initiation into sensualism, an act similar to some of the flamboyantly published stories of the books he read. (*TP*, 23)

He also seemed to get "a sense of thrill of the wrong" (*TP*, 22) from the fact that she was defenseless (*TP*, 22). He began to think of Maria not as a fatherless child worthy of his protection but as a growing girl whom he should, by right, possess (*TP*, 21). He felt that he would be "liberated" (*TP*, 23) after he committed the crime and, thereafter, "live without concern or regret" (*TP*, 23).

Thus, on 5 July 1902, Alessandro devised and enacted a plan to seclude himself with Maria in their peasant farm dwelling. There, as she refused his attempt at rape, he wielded a "brush hook" (*TP*, 49) and "struck her madly, hacking her breast and stomach and back blindingly again and again as though he could slaughter her over and over" (*TP*, 49). He struck her "fourteen times." As the attempt took place, what she saw in her mind (according to DiDonato) was the inscription, "Death, but not sin" (*TP*, 49),[4] the same statement that was in a book, *The Christian Doctrine*, given to her by Alessandro for receiving her first Communion. Tragically, her death occurred the day before her first Communion. (*TP*, 49). As Maria was hit, she, nevertheless utters words of forgiveness and an invitation that was eventually to change Alessandro's life, as will be later shown: "I forgive . . . for you do not know what you are doing. Your soul, . . . Alessandro, I forgive you. I want your soul with me in paradise" (*TP*, 50).[5] On July 5, at 3:45 P.M., Maria Goretti died (*TP*, 73).

Alessandro appeared to have no remorse after the killing (*TP*, 77). He seemed to explain his behavior by saying the killing would not have taken place if Maria "had peacefully submitted to my [his] desire" (*TP*, 81). After impersonally confessing to the killing (*TP*, 89), on 15 October 1902, the court sentenced him to maximum punishment of thirty years, the first three in solitary confinement (*TP*, 95). However, both Maria Goretti and her mother, Assunta, forgave him. When asked for final words in the courtroom at Alessandro's trial, Assunta forgave Alessandro (*TP*, 95). In response, the people as one group in the courtroom angrily objected to Assunta's forgiving words with "Never! It should not be! I would never forgive him" (*TP*, 96). Assunta graciously responded to these people, "And suppose, in turn, Jesus Christ does not forgive us?" (*TP*, 96).

Part 1 of *The Penitent*, containing eight chapters, and the first five chapters of part 2, bring us to the point of the results of Alessandro's trial. Predominantly, part 2 and its remaining ten chapters tell of Alessandro's change to contrition and rebirth.

How did Alessandro's change come about? How would he become penitent for his crime? Most notably, a dream he had of Maria would change his life. His habit of reading would also change him. But there were other influences, other people, especially Maria's mother, Assunta, and her family, who all showed that he could be forgiven for what he had done to Maria. A number of friends also helped him.

First, a dream he had of the girl he murdered would change his life. While Alessandro was in prison, DiDonato tells us, "in [Alessandro's] slumber there was never a dream" (*TP*, 105), until one night a significant dream took place that changed his life for the better (*TP*, 110). Before this dream, each "dragging day" (*TP*, 108) caused "bitterness to gnaw him" (*TP*, 108). Now, in this sleep reverie Maria Goretti appears to him and promises that his soul will be with her in heaven some day (*TP*, 109). DiDonato vividly recounts this moving dream:

> The prison bars and walls fell away and his cell was a sunlit garden blooming with flowers. Toward him came a beautiful girl dressed in pure white. He said to himself, "How is this; peasant girls wear darkish clothes?" But he saw it was Marietta. She was walking among flowers toward him, smiling and without the least fear. He wanted to flee from her, but could not. Marietta picked white lilies and handed them to him, saying, "Alessandro, take them." He accepted the lilies one by one, fourteen of them. But a strange thing took place. As he received them from her fingers, the lilies did not remain lilies but changed into so many splendid flaming lights. There was a lily turned to purifying flame for every one of the fourteen mortal blows he struck her on the fatal day in Ferriere. Marietta said, smiling: "Alessandro, as I have promised, your soul shall some day reach me in heaven." Contentment entered his breast. And the scene of incredible beauty dissolved in silence. (*TP*, 109)

In the "light," Alessandro, for the first time, felt the full horror of what he had done (*TP*, 110). The dream relaxed him and came as a "harbinger of peace" (*TP*, 110, 143). He saw a possibility of meaning in his crime: "Was Marietta chosen for a destiny that transcended her death?" (*TP*, 110).

A religious Sardinian prison friend who had a different sort of dream coaxed Alessandro to believe the dream-vision of Maria: "The soul of the girl you slew came to you in that dream with the message that she seeks to save you. She wants to be your intercessor. You are fortunate, Serenelli, and will be saved" (*TP*, 112). To contrast his state to Alessandro's, the Sardinian told Alessandro of his own dream that his own mother was pursuing him to destroy him (*TP*, 112) because he caught his mother with his own brother betraying his father. As a result, the Sardinian stabbed them both to death (*TP*, 112). The Sardinian's dream was to bring him a different reality than Alessandro's: a few weeks later, the prison guard found the Sardinian dead, hanging from a piece of prison cord (*TP*, 112).

A visit to the prison by the Bishop of Noto, sent by Bishop Tito Cucchi and Cavaliere Marini to "ascertain the state of [Alessandro's] soul" (*TP*, 114) also would contribute to an awareness in Alessandro that Maria Goretti was exercising her "spiritual power" (*TP*, 116) to save him after her death. The Bishop of Noto petitioned Alessandro to save his soul as Maria would want him to (*TP*, 114). Because of the Bishop's visit, Alessandro's world began to be seen as more purposeful: "It was because of Marietta's worth that the Bishop came to him in prison with Christ's love. His heart swelled and new words came from his mouth. . . . I want to cast myself upon God's mercy. I want to beg pardon from the family of [Marietta] whom I destroyed. I want to go on hands and knees before Assunta Goretti and her children for what I have done" (*TP*, 114). He then asked to read Marini's biographical book of Maria Goretti (*TP*, 114–15).

When Alessandro read Marini's book, he was extremely repentant and regretted that he could not have stopped his crime of 5 July 1902. With deep seriousness he read Maria's words of forgiveness of him on the day of her death: "Alessandro, I forgive you—I want your soul with mine in Paradise!" (*TP*, 116). So he drafted a letter of repentance to Bishop Blandini of Noto: "I publicly detest my crime and ask forgiveness from God and also from the poor and desolate family of my victim" (*TP*, 117). Alessandro felt that this book influenced his behavior, but he felt, more importantly, that a "spiritual power" (*TP*, 116) which was to completely transform him was really responsible for his change:

> No, no, not the printed word of an author's own thoughts, but a spiritual power, gave him new, clear eyes and revealed to him his eternal soul, showing that behind in the past was the nightmare of the unbeliever, the killer Alessandro. He felt, he knew, and told himself that the forces transforming him could be no other than the spirit of little Marietta. (*TP*, 116)

This change in Alessandro's life is better understood with DiDonato's interpretation of Alessandro's view of Time: "The element of time metamorphosed into a reasonable entity, an amenable concept . . ." (*TP*, 117). Time becomes not an impersonal force, but a very personal living one: "it would be easier [for Alessandro] to float with the inexplicable mass flow of time as an orderly microscopic person not interfering in the course of any other human being" (*TP*, 119). As mentioned in the chapter on Mother Cabrini's life, *Immigrant Saint*, as Mother Cabrini's use of her time was filled with love, likewise Alessandro's concept of time began to take on a similar meaning and illustrates one of Fr. William F. Lynch's points, that Alessandro now no longer viewed time as meaningless, but as a positive force. Each night Alessandro prayed for

4 / THE PENITENT

Maria's forgiveness (*TP*, 120), and he became a model prisoner (*TP*, 121).

Alessandro's peace also began to grow for other reasons. The same habit of reading that earlier had brought him to his downfall now was to serve as his salvation (*TP*, 184). The prison chaplain, Don Michele, supplied him with many of the books (*TP*, 124–25). He read words of writers who emphasized the theme of salvation (*TP*, 112, 120–24), showing persons who committed evil and were still saved (*TP*, 120–24) and who had cried seriously as he did (*TP*, 120–24). DiDonato tells us that Alessandro read the "Evangelists, Goethe, Dumas, Dante, Manzoni, Bertoldo, Pellico, Dostoyevsky, Tolstoy" (*TP*, 122). DiDonato further says Alessandro enjoyed *The Promised Bride* by Manzoni, because the "murderous brigand" (*TP*, 123) received grace and was saved (*TP*, 123). He enjoyed *Faust*, for he erred, like Alessandro, selling himself to the devil (*TP*, 123). He identified with Dostoyevsky's Raskolnikov's stream-of-conscious thinking (*TP*, 123), and "he wept with joy for the killer's remorse and salvation" (*TP*, 123). According to Dorothee von Huene-Greenberg in an interview, DiDonato found that Alessandro had read and reread a worn and frayed copy of *Crime and Punishment* (*TP*, 41) as well as DiDonato's Italian version of *Christ in Concrete* (*TP*, 179).[6]

As Alessandro served his term he felt that, since having his dream-vision of Maria, there was an "unusual destiny for him to fulfill" (*TP*, 130). "Just what it was, he could not clearly define" (*TP*, 130). He was released under his brother Pietro's care after serving twenty-seven years for good behavior (*TP*, 128, 131). All along, Alessandro felt that it was Marietta's spirit (*TP*, 131) that had released him from prison (*TP*, 131). But wandering from farm to farm as a migrant worker, he had a difficult time after being in prison. People would find out who he was and would shun him (*TP*, 138). An attempt at seduction by a sharecropper's wife also discouraged the repentant Alessandro (*TP*, 139). Like Rip Van Winkle, he had awakened to a different world, where he was "lost and wandering in a mechanical world" (*TP*, 135). Nevertheless, he did his best to cope. He became very sensitive, prayed to Maria and longed to see Assunta, Maria's mother (*TP*, 139–40).

The week before Christmas 1934, Fr. Don Francesco Bernacchio invited Alessandro to Corinaldo, the Goretti family's town of residence, and he also offered Alessandro train fare (*TP*, 141). Alessandro's interaction with Assunta was very positive. She forgave him (*TP*, 142); in addition, her note to him stating that she served as his mother gave him a tremendous amount of hope: "Your evil days are past, and to me you are as a long-suffering son" (*TP*, 142). Celebrating the birth of Christ, he ate dinner with the Goretti family (*TP*, 143) and the next day went to mass with Assunta in the presence of the people of Corinaldo. DiDonato's cinematographic recounting of this compassionate event is warm:

> The next morning, the people of Corinaldo witnessed that which could only happen among the poor of Christ. Assunta Goretti, with head held high and tears falling, took Alessandro Serenelli by the hand as a mother takes a son, and led him to Mass. At the altar rail, side by side, she and he—he who had killed her daughter—raised their open mouths to partake of the flesh and blood of Jesus. (*TP*, 146)

No doubt Fr. Don Bernacchio was also instrumental in helping the penitent Alessandro (*TP*, 151) enter a Capuchin monastery, which initially turned out to be a trying experience. It seems that on a later occasion, a jealous old Capuchin, Mugnetto, accused Alessandro of stealing his four thousand lire. Because of bad publicity resulting from the untrue charge, Alessandro was finally released from the monastery (*TP*, 154). In time, however, he received two other offers to join religious orders, one from the Passionists of San Marcella, the postulants of Maria Goretti's sainthood, and the other from the Capuchins (*TP*, 154). Don Bernacchio counseled him to choose another monastery of the Capuchin order rather than that of the Passionists, since they were postulating Maria for sainthood (*TP*, 154). As the canonization of Maria Goretti proceeded to take place (she was Beatified 27 April 1947 and canonized 24 June 1950 [*TP*, 158]), Alessandro became ever more penitent as he describes in a letter to his brother, Pietro: "The feast of Marietta's beatification in Rome was also a profound and festive rejoicing for my penitent soul" (*TP*, 159).

DiDonato shows that Assunta's "maternal love" (*TP*, 162) was to prove instrumental in the salvation of this motherless former killer. It appears that Alessandro took on a Mother component in Assunta, to use the Jungian vocabulary, and this contributed to his development, to the development of his female component.[7] Alessandro again became part of the forgiving Goretti family, often visiting, talking with, cooking with, and helping both Ersilia, Assunta's sister, and Assunta (*TP*, 162). He would return to them believing that his life now had a mission (*TP*, 162; chap. 12). As Assunta requested a photograph that included Alessandro, a rare occurrence in an Italian family, she uttered words that were surely curing words to Alessandro, "Am I not your mother, Alessandro? Well, then, come closer to me" (*TP*, 163). On 8 October, in his monastery, he received the message that he was to come to see her, as she was dying and had requested his presence (*TP*, 164). Father Valentine found him "weeping, helpless" (*TP*, 165) and exhorted him to "gratefully accept what God wills" (*TP*, 165). DiDonato poignantly describes Alessandro's initial reaction to the news that Assunta was dying:

> The staunchest of womankind, the mother of forgiveness, the mother like Mary, the only mother for him and his battered life, was leaving him. Fear and weakness overcame him. Without her warmth, commiseration and encouraging smile his world would be field without the sun. He turned to the altar and prayed that Assunta would live yet a while. (*TP*, 164)

But he was never to see Assunta alive again; he arrived after she died, and heard her sister Ersilia say, "Uncle Alessandro—be strong now—Mamma dearest is dead" (*TP*, 165). At her deathbed, Alessandro "cried aloud, 'Mamma'" (*TP*, 166), and he repeated sobbingly all night, "Dearest Mamma . . . Assunta . . . Mamma, Mamma!" (*TP*, 160).

Alessandro returned to the monastery to retire, where he read often and thought of Maria (*TP*, 166). He ended his days, praying most tearfully at night, with his rosary by his candlelighted picture of Maria: "Marietta, I wait for death. Marietta, I await and long for fulfillment of your promise that I will be by your side in Paradise, Marietta" (*TP*, 166).

DiDonato's own words, spoken during an interview (*DIOM*, 104–5, 113–14), are indeed an exemplification of the positive changes made in Alessandro's life: love can shame death and life takes place in a mystery,[8] which is love. Maria Goretti's promise to save Alessandro probably did save him. Other influences also affected him, but all of them, to Alessandro, represented love. This change in Alessandro was a far cry from his thinking in the hot marshes on the day he took St. Maria Goretti's life. Though DiDonato's early statement indicated that "fate had conspired against Alessandro . . . to be without a mother and family" (*TP*, 16), that fate was to take on positive meaning because of the love of Maria Goretti and her family. Alessandro acquired the courage (male component) to face the future with love and hope (female component). When Alessandro had seen how the movie industry had portrayed a negative image of his father in a film on the Goretti murder, he said, "Poor father! He did not deserve that" (*TP*, 186). This sensitivity for others and the growth embodied in the male and female components were brought about by the power (mystery) of hope, love and faith—indeed, for Alessandro, life now had become sacred and filled with love.

Finally, it is not coincidence that DiDonato prefixes part 2, "Repentance," with a quotation from 2 Corinthians 5.17: "For the grief that is according to God worketh repentance without regret, unto salvation..." (*TP*, 75).

5
"Christ in Plastic"

As indicated in chapter 2, Pietro DiDonato described himself in interviews as a social and political protester, who was filled with "rebellion" (*DIOM*, 101). His personal communications support the impressions of his books that he had an intense sense of social justice and a sympathy for the oppressed (*CC, TCOL*).[1] The same sensibility is apparent in "Christ in Plastic," published in *Penthouse* in 1978, a narrative diary-essay based on the assassination of Aldo Moro. President of the Christian Democrats, Italy's ruling party at the time, Moro was killed by the BR (*Brigate Rosse*) or the Red Brigade, a revolutionary group seeking justice. DiDonato's essay is an exciting, though gruesome, account of Moro's death, including the reasons for that murder. Michael Esposito's interview[2] leads us to believe that DiDonato's sympathy was with the BR. On 8 May 8 1978, Moro, held captive by the BR, was killed when the government refused "to exchange thirteen terrorist leaders for him" (*CIP*, 75). The ability of DiDonato to create from whatever has already occurred in the past, including information gathered from interviews as he did previously in *The Immigrant Saint: The Life of Mother Cabrini* and *The Penitent*, makes him an excellent chronicler.

The background, genesis and choice of title of "Christ in Plastic" provides important and interesting information to the understanding of the essay. Concerning its genesis, DiDonato was asked to write the article by John Lombardi, an editor who came from *Esquire* to *Penthouse* a week before Moro's body was found. When Moro's body was found, Lombardi called and asked DiDonato to go to Rome to do the story.[3] DiDonato had traveled often to Italy and knew two revolutionaries, whom he labeled "R1" and "R2" (*CIP*, 76). R2 was instrumental in furnishing access to the cell—a group of terrorists that kidnapped and murdered Moro (*CIP*, 76). So DiDonato left for Italy, as he mentions in the preface, to write the story: "I spent two months interviewing the two Brigasti [R1 and R2, mentioned above], friends of the Moro family, police, journalists, political observers, priests—whoever would talk to me. From the material I gathered I allowed myself the license to portray Moro's fifty-four-day ordeal and crucifixion" (*CIP*, 76).

When Michael Esposito asked DiDonato whether the title, "Christ in Plastic," favored the Red Brigade, DiDonato responded, "I did not give it that title."[4] DiDonato's own choice for the title was first "RB."[5] Nevertheless, DiDonato does mention that he empathized with the Red Brigade.[6] DiDonato went on to say that John Lombardi gave it that title "by trading in . . . on my well-known book, *Christ in Concrete*. I didn't give any opposition. I didn't care."[7] He continued that he was trying to write "the truth."[8]

When Dorothee von Huene-Greenberg asked DiDonato what he thought he was bringing to the world as a missionary, he replied, "truth."[9] DiDonato also mentioned that the executioners of Moro wrapped him in "opaque plastic" (*CIP*, 62) after they had killed him.

The essay is written as a predominantly third-person journalistic diary account of the doings of the Red Brigade, beginning with the place and date of "Rome, March 16, 1978" (*CIP*, 76), and continuing with chronological headings of twenty-two other dates, the last one being "May 9." Amidst the seriousness of tone and the portrayal of several violent scenes, DiDonato has the ability to seed these accounts with satirical, humorous, almost absurd portrayals of reality (as he did in the unpublished novel, "The Gospels," which he gave to me). For instance, under "May 1," Magistrate Mario Daniele suggests commuting the sentences of all BR prisoners to two years in exchange for Moro (*CIP*, 229); DiDonato writes the following, noting the various responses to Daniele's request:

> Zacagnini [the Christian Democratic Secretary, onetime friend of Moro], no doubt thinking of Nostradamus, thunders "No!" again.
>
> Yassir Arafat defines the BR terrorists as "military operations."
>
> Idi Amin Dada, over Radio Kampala in Uganda, says he will convince the BR to release Moro, since he believes, along with Jimmy Carter, in upholding human rights. . . .
>
> President Carter's representative, Joe Califano, who doesn't know his ass from a hole in the ground in Italy, applauds Zacagnini's "No." (*CIP*, 229)

The frustration with the futility of the happenings surrounding Moro's kidnapping is manifested in DiDonato's depiction of the absurdity of reality. The staccato, journalistic, third-person style proves effective in depicting gruesome events, often reminding one of Ernest Hemingway's style:

> Franco and Anna [Red Brigade members] get out. He holds a 9mm. pistol; she, a Scorpion machine pistol. Both are fitted with silencers. They lift the station wagon's rear door and fix the latch. Moro looks at them. To die in such a shabby way . . .
>
> Eleven bullets slam through Moro's chest, leaving a path of punctures. They wrap him in a large sheet of orange-colored plastic and place him on a heavy, soiled overcoat. They put their guns in a STANDA store bag and drive back onto the highway toward Rome. (*CIP*, 231)

The seemingly casual tone of this scene reinforces the obvious violence.

But what more can we say of the sustaining plot that weaves these terrorists' incidents together? Why was Moro kidnapped? How were he and the reigning Christian Democrat Party viewed by the Red Brigade of the people and, ultimately, how was Moro viewed as he approached his murder? In addition, how can we reconcile the plot with DiDonato's previous statement that he empathized with the BR?[10] How will the narrative movement of the essay increase our understanding of the real meaning behind that interesting title, "Christ in Plastic"?

First, in order to understand some of the questions above, we might well consider two incidents in *Christ in Concrete*. The first incident occurs when Paolo crushes a crucifix made of "a plaster man and wood" (*CC*, 304) in the presence and to the dismay of his mother (*CC*, 304). Paolo does this because he feels an "injustice" (*CC*, 314) has been done to him, for his father's death will be used "against him" (*CC*, 303) in life. A crucifix made of plaster of paris and wood is not real—it is artificial and not strong like concrete. The second incident occurs when Paul, sometimes referred to as Paolo, goes to the police station to find out if his father has been found after the collapse that kills him. The response of the policeman is cold, distant and inconsiderate of Paul's presence. The parallel of "wrapping paper" (*CC*, 40) to "plastic" in "Christ in Plastic" is interesting. Paper or plastic is not concrete. The policeman yells out, "What?—Oh, yeah—the Wop [Geremio] is under the wrappin' paper out in the courtyard!" (*CC*, 40). To DiDonato, the work his father did with concrete represented hard, honest work, quite the opposite of Moro's regime. Both the plastic wrapping of Moro in "Christ in Plastic" and the phrase "wrappin' paper" in *Christ in Concrete* used by the policeman represent the antithesis of "concrete," what

Paolo's father manifested in his work in construction: justice, hard work, love, endurance, courage and genuineness. In contrast, what does Moro and his government represent in "Christ in Plastic"? Quite unlike Paolo's father's work, Moro and his government represent the artificial, the injustice of life as depicted by the Red Brigade (*CIP*, 80, 222), by Aniello Coppola's biography of Moro (*CIP*, 222), by DiDonato himself (*CIP*, 80, 224), and, finally, by Moro himself in his last desperate moments before his death (*CIP*, 226). The thirty years of Moro's political rule are characterized as a "manipulation of Italy" (*CIP*, 222) and Italians (*CIP*, 222), for Moro was silent "about Vietnam, Chile and South American dictatorships manufactured in the White House" (*CIP*, 222). "Worse, [Moro's government] had loused up Italy" (*CIP*, 224). Zucor, a Red Brigade member, blames Moro and his government for the death of Feltrinelli, a champion of the worker, and Zucor lashes out, characterizing Moro as the brains of the "Catholic and dollar democratic hierarchy" (*CIP*, 233). Later, as Moro pleads to the government to save his life, his own political party abandons him (*CIP*, 224): "When Moro becomes more desperate with the refusal of his friends to bargain with the BR to save his life, he even accuses them along with himself: 'You—Saccagini, Andreotti, Fanfani, Berlinguer, Leone and Cossiga—are all guilty along with me and must rise to the manliness of my fate'" (*CIP*, 226).

Moro's petition was never fulfilled. On "April 24" the BR makes its final appeal to exchange thirteen prisoners for Moro's life (*CIP*, 226). Fearing the consequences of bargaining with hostages and desiring to profit from political motives (*CIP*, 229), the government and religious officials do not release Moro. The Christian Democrats even herald the martyrdom of Moro (*CIP*, 230) as Moro becomes even more furious, saying he does not want these "men of power" (*CIP*, 229) and the Pope at his funeral (*CIP*, 229). Finally, Moro is killed and wrapped in plastic (*CIP*, 231).

It appears to this author that according to DiDonato, the Red Brigade deserve empathy, for they are portrayed as the oppressed in "Christ in Plastic." This empathy can be borne out in Esposito's interview:

> As for my supporting the activities of the Red Brigade, I see the justification of their ideals and of their activities. My function is that of an observer, like Dante in hell. I would rather show empathy for them than for the current government, but the way I feel is the way a majority of Italians in Italy feel. They told me confidentially in the streets and in their homes: "We need the Red Brigade. We're sick of the cor-

ruption. We're sick of the police state, of police brutality." Yes, I do support the Red Brigade.[11]

In addition, DiDonato's introductory comments in "Christ in Plastic" characterize Aldo Moro as a "synthetic savior of the Christian Democrats, the crucified politician, the modern plastic Christ" (*CIP*, 76). DiDonato seems to say, in "Christ in Plastic," that Moro is a martyr, but not a martyr who stands for the justice that a government or political party should represent.

It is interesting to note that in DiDonato's *The Penitent*, Cardinal Salvotti, postulating sainthood for a Bavarian girl, uses St. Thomas's axiom that a martyr is one who "chooses to die in defense of even a single Christian precept" (*TP*, 147). Pope Pius then suggests Marietta Goretti was another candidate for Sainthood (*TP*, 147–48). It is clear to the Red Brigade and to DiDonato that in no way was Moro destined for sainthood in "Christ in Plastic." Hence the emphasis on the words "plastic" and "synthetic," opposite to "concrete," their contrariety, is representative of the commendable work values of Paul's own father, Geremio, in *Christ in Concrete*.

Though DiDonato tends to favor the Red Brigade, he also warns the Red Brigade that they, too, can become "robots," as the Nazi and Fascists gradually became.[12] In response to this warning of DiDonato, some Red Brigades answered, "We are the idealists because we must know, and tell, the truth to respect ourselves. We jeopardize our lives for the future because it's an answer to the negativity and degeneration of man. We know what man can be. . . . Man can be better."[13] Being idealistic like the Red Brigade, DiDonato seems to have identified with them: "Everything dies. Life is essentially a tragedy, but the person with ideals can muster the courage to face death. I can face the mystery of death better as an idealist. That's why I write; it's an outlet for me."[14]

Hence, in writing "Christ in Plastic," DiDonato was exemplifying his own sense of "protest," "rebellion," and "injustice" (*DIOM*, 101) as he pursued the truth about Moro's death. The "love" one has for what one does and for what one believes in can "shame death" (*DIOM*, 105). DiDonato's pursuit of a sense of justice against evil therefore manifests itself both in his writing and life. In his works and interviews, DiDonato often concerned himself with justice, truth and oppression[15] (*CC, CIP, DIOM*), as he also did when he showed us Moro's world of "plastic," which represented the social, political, economic injustices of power.

What we might see in the Red Brigade's relation to political reform is that it embodies both the male and female virtues so touted by Jung. The sensitive reaching out for social justice is, in Schopenhauer's sense, a feminine gesture—as Schopenhauer shows in his selection of Christ and Socrates to demonstrate the feminine practice of virtue. On the other hand, the Red Brigade's willingness to use violence to gain their ends is what Schopenhauer would dub the masculine virtue. Thus, this coupling serves to illustrate Jung's thesis that both male and female virtues interact.

6
The Love of Annunziata

In chapter 2 in this study, the author commented that Pietro DiDonato told him that no matter what we do, it takes in mystery, containing elements of love and sacredness that have the power to overcome death (*DIOM*, 105). *The Love of Annunziata* is about death and life and the forgiveness that comes out of love. It is about Geremio, Paul's father, and about Geremio's wife, Annunziata. Love does shame death in this play. In addition, this drama of love takes place in an atmosphere of mystery. The word "mystery" also appears repeatedly in the play.

The mystery that occurs in the play has several levels of meaning. First, a very important sense of foreshadowing, occurring in a dreamlike atmosphere, and the many references to threes, or a trinity, both secular and religious, create suspense. The religious mystery of the Crucifixion on Good Friday when Annunziata mentions the Trinity (*LOA*, 131; scene 2) to Paul, her son, is connected in a mysterious fashion to the foreshadowing of Geremio's own death, which occurs at a construction site, also on Good Friday. In another sense, the mystery of Annunziata's forgiveness of Geremio's infidelity is most crucial, for it depicts Christ's own forgiveness of man, including those who persecuted Him, as part of the fulfillment of the mystery of the Trinity. This love of Christ who came to die that we might forgive and love, especially those who injure us,[1] culminates for Annunziata in her forgiveness of and love for Geremio as he returns home on Easter (scene 3). Her mention at his funeral of the coming birth of their child is an expression of love that reminds one of the mystery of the Nativity. Since the play takes place in an atmosphere of the dreamlike world, it also features a dreamlike dance of the robust tarantella by Annunziata in a theater (scene 3) and in Annunziata's realistic preparation for childbirth (scene 3). Thematically, the play is about a genuine triumph over death and forgiveness over death. The desire of Geremio to take his wife to the theater in the early scenes is fulfilled later in scene 3 in

Annunziata's mind as she reenacts the tarantella, for in the mystery of her mind she has forgiven and loved Geremio. All scenes lead to the culmination and the mystery of the dance of the Tarantella of Annunziata and Geremio. The intertwining of religious and realistic world elements unifies the play's movements.

The atmosphere of the play is set in all three scenes, occurring respectively on Holy Thursday, Good Friday, and Easter Sunday. In scene 1, Geremio wants to go to the theater to see a Valentino movie, but his wife wants him to remain home. Geremio, instead, does stay home. The next day Geremio goes to work on Good Friday (scene 2). At work, he dies by falling off a work scaffold (scene 2). Then he returns "home" in scene 3 in a coffin at his funeral. However, in Annunziata's mind he reappears on stage in a theater at a party for him as she desires to dance with him. This atmosphere of an unreal, dreamlike mystery of a "resurrection" about to occur in Annunziata's mind, is also present in all scenes of the play.

The play opens with Geremio's exclamation in scene 1: "What mystery! This life *is* fantastic! What phenomena!" (121). This statement comes as Geremio hears Paul's newly constructed radio. Like a wireless radio, parts of the play transmit messages in an atmosphere of mystery, at times foretelling future incidents. On Good Friday, Paul responds to his mother's talk about the Trinity with "Holy smokes, what's all this mystery?" (131, scene 3). In scene 3 Grazia forecasts the funeral of Geremio: "Annunziata, child, now has come for you a strange moment" (132). To Annunziata, Geremio comes home a "stranger" (scene 3). Later, at the funeral, Annunziata admits she is "beset by signs and dreams" (scene 3), and she also asks, "Where did I dream you whistled for help?" (136, scene 3) as she contemplates his moment of death. Also at the funeral, Annunziata, "like being in a dream" (138, scene 3), proposes to dance with Geremio, who in her mind has "come alive" or been "resurrected," or, in fact, has returned "home."[2] The return to "home" emphasizes, on the most literal level, death. On another level, Geremio's prediction or foreshadowing of his death, as will be shown, is fulfilled and a "resurrection" occurs on this Easter Sunday, for he "comes alive" in the theater of Annunziata's mind to be forgiven and loved in Annunziata's "life-in-death" dance.

What will be discussed, then, are several incidents which foreshadow scene 3, and then what the author sees as the ultimate message and meaning of the play, primarily the compassionate forgiveness and love of Annunziata, which is also demonstrated at Geremio's death, especially in scene 3.

First, a number of interesting, specific occurrences foreshadow the death of Geremio. Mrs. Farrell, a neighbor of Geremio's family, acts as a harbinger of death in scene 1. Her statement to Annunziata is quite fatalistic and predictive of Geremio's death: "Well, ain't no arguing with your star. The road's marked out an' you can't whangle it" (127). As Geremio gives Mrs. Farrell a glass of wine, she says, "Yes, let's drink it before we die!" (127). She then tells of a neighbor's funeral and says funerals occur in "threes." Mrs. Farrell mentions two more funerals, and as she does this, DiDonato tells us about the effect she has on Geremio and Annunziata.

> [GEREMIO's *face is getting darker.* ANNUNZIATA, *looking at him is more pale; and his eyes, gazing into hers, are burning.* MRS. FARRELL *places her thick hand on* GEREMIO's *shoulder and croaks*] Mister, Gawd forbid, but when any of you die . . . [GEREMIO's *glass slips from his hand. When it crashes on the floor* ANNUNZIATA *almost screams. . . .*]
> (*LOA*, 128)

Mrs. Farrell is also connected to two references made to Easter and Christmas. These holidays represent in the play the "resurrection" of Geremio in Annunziata's mind, the forgiveness of Geremio by Annunziata. Christmas represents the idea that after Geremio's death, his offspring will be born to continue his legacy (scene 3). At Mrs. Farrell's first appearance in the play, she says to Paulie, who is listening to the radio, "Did you hear anythin' from Sanny Closs?" (125, scene 1). Later, Geremio gives Mrs. Farrell a gallon of wine and says, "For you. A—Christmas—I mean—Easter present" (128). These Christian holidays are not mentioned haphazardly. Geremio will die on Good Friday, and "rise" in scene 3 in Annunziata's mind—Easter. In another sense, his sacrifice will live in the nativity of his own offspring—Christmas—as pregnant Annunziata says at his funeral, "The blood of Geremio seeks life" (138). The fusion of death (the funeral scene) and the dance of Annunziata (Easter; resurrection) and the prediction of birth (Christmas) are craftily interwoven into the liturgy and movement of the play, pointing to the theme of the play, that magnanimous *love* of Annunziata for her husband, as will be shown later.

Another instance of foreshadowing of the death of Geremio and the events of scene 3 is indicated by Geremio himself, previous to the appearance of Mrs. Farrell. When Annunziata refuses Geremio's request to go to the theater to see Valentino, Geremio says, "Come, I have promised myself these days to have you and me at theater when the

Valentino plays" (123, scene 3). As Geremio playacts in front of the children, and Annunziata exchanges playful comments with him, he sets the stage for the prediction of the funeral-theater-dance scene (scene 3).

> GEREMIO: I'll depart mi-lady too-too superb, *but*, I'll take this bricklaying Gerrrr-e-mmio—the—r-r-rat away from you someday! I'll visit you in a manner so ceremonious, so fantastic, that you will not deny me![3]
>
> ANNUNZIATA: But sure—sure—
>
> GEREMIO: [Brushing an imaginary mustachio, he bows]: When I come I shall seduce you so—so completely you won't know the time of day. You'll regret what you've said, little peasant [said playfully] when you hear the grand music, when you see the carriages, the attendants, you'll regret; the pomp! the fanfare! Ahhh-h how you'll regret! Ta-rah-ta-rahhh! Here comes Don Geremio! Ta-rah-ta-rahh!
>
> (scene 1)

As the children giggle, and they prepare to draw the wine, Annunziata perceives Geremio's words as a mystery:

> ANNUNZIATA: [*she suddenly ceases to smile. She is ominously pensive. Her mouth falls open and as an echo she repeats*]: Carriages?! Attendants? . . ."
>
> (scene 1)

At another point, Geremio also foreshadows his own death and return that will occur in scene 3: "Let children's voices be my music. Let always my wife, be my inamorata. Let *home* be my Paradise" (129, scene 1). Incidentally, this music of Geremio's children will become his son Paul's peace and triumph at the end of *This Woman*, another novel of DiDonato, as Paul plays with his child on the beach in his pregnant wife's presence. In scene 3 of *The Love of Annunziata*, the emphasis that Geremio has come "home" is most evident, as reported by Annunziata (136), Regina (134) and Maria (133). In scene 3 (131–32), Paul also says, "Papa is home," after he hears three whistles that occur on Good Friday, representing the Crucifixion of Christ and the death-fall of his father from the work scaffold at 3 P.M.

Other occurrences, relating to the sound of these three whistles seemingly made by Geremio, foreshadow Geremio's death and the occurrences of scene 3. On Good Friday, while Geremio goes to work, pregnant Annunziata hears three whistles as she makes an Easter cake with the symbolic cross of dough. She experiences a "quick pain" (130, scene 2) in her stomach. She goes on to bless the cake as the bells of San Rocco ring (131). Mentioning the words of the Trinity, she finishes blessing the cake as Paul comes in and sees her crying. At this time, Annunziata tries to explain to Paul the mystery of the Crucifixion: "Son, it is actually at this time that our Lord Jesus was fixed to the cross" (131, scene 2). Young Paul insists, "If we were there we could've saved Him!" (131, scene 2). He also mentions that "Papa is home" (131, scene 2), and Annunziata, fearing the worst tragedy for Geremio, and "trembling and her eyes widening" (121, scene 2), asks, "Why?" . . . (131, scene 2). Paul then tells her of the whistles: "I was just about to step into Saint Rocco's, and Papa wanted me; he whistled from the window here three times to me" (132, scene 2). Then we anticipate what we know will be the announcement of Geremio's death. Paul warns us that he hears something outside the apartment:

> Mother, I hear a lot of feet in the hallway. *[He walks to the hallway door, always looking at her]* Mother . . . there's people outside the door . . . [ANNUNZIATA *grips the arm rest, her jaws tighten, she pushes her head back against the rocker, and holds her breath, staring. There is a soft, respectful knock on the door.*]
> (132, scene 2)

At this point we realize the announcement of Geremio's death is imminent.

The message and meaning of the play are reinforced in the funeral scene of Geremio in scene 3 through Annunziata's "life-in-death" dance. This dance most represents a tremendous resurrection of feeling on her part: in short, a compassion and a forgiveness of and love for Geremio. When Geremio returns "home" and "rises" (comes alive and is symbolically forgiven) in Annunziata's mind, the message of Annunziata's love surmounts his death (the sin of Geremio, also). This "resurrection" represents Annunziata's forgiveness and love (life). In order for us to understand the magnanimous love of this Italian woman, we must first understand the sin that guilty Geremio confesses to her.

Annunziata understands the shortcomings of men and forgives, despite Geremio's sin, for she is very Christlike. In scene 1, Geremio confesses his sin of betrayal:

GEREMIO: And tonight I . . . I feel, I *know*, I might have been a better husband, a better father . . .

ANNUNZIATA: No one can be better than thee.

GEREMIO: Dear one, I *have* been unfaithful. Many times. I have sullied thee with taste and touch of strange women.

ANNUNZIATA: You are mine.

GEREMIO [*Looking into her face*]: Do you know I have always lied to thee and sought the fruit of women beyond my home? That I am the buffoon who never thought of wife? That the heart of Geremio lived and dreamed among the whoring skirts?

ANNUNZIATA: I don't care what you say . . . you are Geremio. . .

GEREMIO: Do you know I have always used you, and played and played you, and have been the peacock and not the husband? Do you —

ANNUNZIATA: If you have hurt me, it was the dear sweet hurt.
(129, scene 2)

In scene 3, Geremio's coffin is brought into a theater while funeral music plays in the background. In this scene, Annunziata actually demonstrates publicly her tremendous love of and forgiveness for Geremio in the dance of the tarantella. After the Paesanos place the coffin on the bier, Annunziata "sees" (imagines) Geremio coming down the aisle as a "haughty" but "ashamed" dancer (scene 3). First, she perceives him as a "stranger," and then she starts mumbling words of praise to him, dumbfounding all the others at the funeral (135, scene 3). For her, Geremio cannot die: "Is this a trick? — Why do you [Geremio] play with me so? . . . It is wonderful of you to surprise me with this party and to have invited the Paesans without my knowing" (135–36; scene 3). In her resplendent surprise and joy, Annunziata again recognizes and mentions the sins that Geremio has committed, but she rises above them and forgives him a second time, just before starting to dance the tarantella: "And of course, my dancing husband, you might, as usual, have been playing Italian sport 'mongst the loose legs of your precious American women of the short hair and skirts—no matter—no offense—it's understood you are man" (136, scene 3). Annunziata is presented as very human here, and very compassionate, for she understands that

Geremio is only "man," and he, too, errs. In accepting and forgiving Geremio's sin, Annunziata displays Christ-like love. In accepting Geremio, she also recalls the mysterious whistles of scene 2:

> And I did think you were gone so, so long. You must forgive me as one without schooling from the old country who is beset by signs and dreams, but Geremio, where did I dream you whistled for help—do not be angry with me, please—and then was it not told me so very strangely you were prevented from coming home?
> (136, scene 3)

On its most literal level, to be "prevented" from coming home is merely to die. But to be forgiven and to be resurrected in Annunziata's mind is to allow Geremio to come home: "It is wonderful of you to surprise me with this party. He has come home" (136, scene 3).

Annunziata's final appearance in the dance scene at the funeral indicates her resolve to forgive Geremio. This scene is a vital part of the play that demonstrates to the author that before a person lives, he must die[4] to any hate within himself that results from the transgression and wrong of another's sin. The analogy to breathing and dancing as opposed to remaining "still" (138, scene 3) in sorrow illustrates the difference between "finding" oneself or "losing" oneself. Annunziata's words demonstrate her desire to love and forgive and to forget Geremio's sin. For Geremio, to return "home" is to be forgiven.

> You promised to take me to see the Valentino; tell me, whom did you bring? Did something happen? You must be careful—I could not breathe if something happened to you—Yet you've tried my patience—Why were you unfaithful? But you have returned! Oh, I feel I must dance—or are you tired! Just this once! Remember, it was at the dance of Carnival where first we met—I must dance or I can't breathe!—Like being in a dream where—I must—must! I lift myself! Oh, Geremio, I will suffocate if I remain still—I must dance or lose myself!! [GEREMIO *smiles roué-ishly.* ANNUNZIATA, *with great excitement*] Quick, Geremio, we must dance! Dance! Dance!
> (138)

Annunziata's forgiveness of and love for Geremio in *The Love of Annunziata* is similar to that displayed for Geremio in *Three Circles of Light* (*TCOL*, 2–3, 244);[5] however, it must also be said that in the novel *Three Circles*, Annunziata also displays more anger and hate toward Geremio for his womanizing and betrayal (*TCOL*, 236, 237).

Nevertheless, in *The Love of Annunziata,* the play, Annunziata also demonstrates another level of forgiveness that is even greater than that of her Paesanos. Even though Annunziata knows, in *The Love,* that Geremio has been adulterous with "American women" (*LOA,* 136, scene 3), she forgives him in the face of the Paesanos, who do not as readily forgive him, since they see Geremio's attempt to have a relationship with American women as an attempt to "pass" as an American rather than as an Italian.

> If they [Paesanos] choose to call you haughty and American, so what—
> 'Tis an honor—I am proud—and we can always make counter-evil-eye without their noticing. . . .
>
> (136, scene 3)

Like the Paesanos of *Three Circles,* both Rose Basile Green and Barbara Gae Bauer see Geremio's attempt to "pass" as an American in *Three Circles* as his downfall, a tragic flaw that will prove the wages of sin is death.[6] The nature of Geremio's sin may also account for the reason why Geremio feels victimized in his suffering, like a clown being derided (*LOA,* 129, scene 1; *CC,* 298).[7] As has been shown in the chapter on *Three Circles,* Geremio's sin of betrayal is emphasized much more in *Three Circles* than in *The Love of Annunziata* because the love of Annunziata is more heavily emphasized in the play.

In conclusion, DiDonato's emphasis in *The Love of Annunziata* upon the use of "threes," the Trinity, and in the creation of a sense that life takes place in a "mystery," coupled with Annunziata's dreamlike visions, which ultimately result in her tarantella "life-in-death" dance, create a tightly constructed drama. Its most significant message is the magnanimous love and forgiveness of an Italian woman for her husband. The play is not without its religious significance. Bauer also maintains that little has been said of DiDonato as a religious artist writing novels.[8] She believes DiDonato's works indicate "his achievement as a religious novelist."[9] In addition, the author feels that the play, *The Love of Annunziata,* can also be considered most religious in spirit. Annunziata's dreamlike visions serve a purpose in the play: they demonstrate her love. Despite this love we are presented with the reality that Geremio has sinned, has experienced his guilt, confesses it and has to agonizingly live with it. Without Annunziata's presence in Paul's life, it is the author's belief that things may not have gone as well for him as they seem to do at the end of another of DiDonato's novels, *This Woman,* where Paul seems to arrive at manhood, as I try to show in the next chapter. This growth of Paul in *This Woman* comes through tremendous agony[10] and with his development of the female component which certainly was related to the love his mother demonstrated in her life and in this play.

In addition, like Henry James's novels, where characters can represent social motifs or values, possibly Annunziata's love and acceptance can represent a respect for the attempt on Geremio's part for a final ethnic acceptance of the American experience, whereas Geremio's guilt, on the other hand, may represent the Paesanos' reluctance to become acculturated as Americans.

7

This Woman

Pietro DiDonato said that love can shame death (*DIOM*, 105) and that love can take place in a sacredness and mystery (*DIOM*, 104–5, 113–14; *TW*, 195).

This Woman, a novel published in 1959, illustrates how a married couple, Isa and Paolo di Alba, come to accept themselves through much agony. Isa comes to terms with the death of her first husband, Jack Tromm, and the antipathy displayed by her second husband, Paolo di Alba, toward her first marriage relationship as well as her relationships with other men. Paolo eventually comes to terms with his love/hate relationship with Isa. However, at first, Paolo seems to be obsessed with the fact that others have had sex with or been married to Isa. Any reminders of these past relationships set Paolo off into a frenzy. Barbara Gae Bauer feels that the ending of the novel does not have a resolution, that it contradicts other parts of the novel, and that it is not convincing.[1] This author disagrees with these statements. Furthermore, not many other writers have spoken more positively and prominently of this novel. Rose Basile Green, however, does feel that Paolo does mature at the end of the novel,[2] though she also says, "Aesthetically, this book is disturbing and unbalanced."[3] The author believes that, though this book is complex, it has a balance in the sense that the characters' difficulties are resolved with some sense of reality. Another critic, Michael Esposito, calls *This Woman* "a sexual potboiler."[4] On the other hand, I think the novel is more artistically redeeming than that; in fact that it is a key novel to the understanding of the whole corpus of Pietro DiDonato's fiction and longer drama. It may very well be his best novel.

The resolution of the novel can be described as the self-discovery of Isa and Paolo. But before they can love each other, they must first undergo the experience that Paolo, also referred to as Paul, talks of at the end of the novel: "It was a life where certain roads had to be travelled alone" (*TW*, 213). "And alone in aloneness man meets his Soul" (*TW*, 215). Both Isa and Paolo must die to the evil[5] within themselves to live fully—to find their "Soul" (*TW*, 220). The past, which was impeding their growth needed to be resolved. To Dorothee von Huene-Greenberg, DiDonato once said, "We must turn our backs on the past. The past is bad, most of it" (50). Both Isa and Paolo must die to the past that is holding them back from living in the present. The journey "alone" (*TW*, 213) is the journey of resolving self-conflict. In an interview with the author, DiDonato said, "The only God that I have now is beauty and my wife" (*DIOM*, 100).

This Woman, the author feels, is an agonizingly serious search for the woman of DiDonato's life and his search for the "flower of womankind" (*CC*, 310–11), and the depth and creativity of the novel remind him of similar qualities found in William Faulkner's works. *This Woman*, then, is a turbulent love/hate novel about Paolo di Alba and his wife, Isa. As previously said, it speaks of their terror and the resolution of this terror that results in self-discovery. Both characters accept themselves and self-identity when they "die" to something within themselves which is holding them back from growth or from love. Through the interesting death imagery and symbolism of Pluto's underworld, the environs of Skittara Cemetery and a mental asylum, DiDonato shows that Isa and Paul discover "Soul" (*TW*, 220), the life force within themselves. It is only then that Paolo, as well as Isa, can come "home" to some sense that comes through forgiveness and mature insight. We found that, in *The Love of Annunziata*, DiDonato's play, to come "home" meant to love and forgive, especially as exemplified by Geremio's wife, Annunziata. In *This Woman*, much forgiving takes place so that Paolo and Isa can "come home."

The resolution of the novel takes place in the context of finding a "home." The wish/prediction of finding home made by Annunziata in *Christ in Concrete* for her son is fulfilled in *This Woman*:

> Son . . . everything in my world is for thee. For thee I desire the fullest gifts of Heaven. To thee must the good Dio bestow the world and lasting health. He must bless thee with the flower of womankind and many-many children as yourself . . . and joy and peace without measure—for to me—thou art most precious. (*CC*, 310–11)

In *This Woman*, Isa and Paolo have only one child with each other. With another child on its way, they will become closer to each other.

These children become part of the resolution of the novel, as depicted in the final scene, where Paolo plays with his young child on the beach in the presence of his wife (*TW*, 220).

However, the resolution cannot occur until the turbulent moments of the novel are resolved. Paolo gives us a pivotal line that will help us understand what will have to take place before a climax and resolution occur: "Isa held the key [to sanity] with her dead husband" (*TW*, 180). Both Isa and Paolo have to cast off their "guilt," anger and hate to discover themselves and each other. Eventually, Paolo will find that he cannot possess a woman, and Isa will find that she was Isa Latham (her maiden name), not Isa Tromm or Isa di Alba (both her first and second husbands' surnames). In this self-discovery, Isa Tromm will remember her past (*TW*, 201, 211), but she eventually will accept that past and go forward with her future life with Paolo. At one point Paolo tells us of his agony of the past: "How did one change, obliterate, remake the past? It was more real than the present: it remained in the constant mind" (*TW*, 131). Both Isa and Paolo need to live with their pasts before they can find their future.

Before love can shame death and before life can occur in a mystery of sacredness (see also Isa's statement, *TW*, 195),[6] both Isa and Paolo will undergo much pain. Once Isa and Paolo eliminate the "skeletons in their closets," they become more whole, more resigned to living in the future. In her search for self-discovery, Isa ironically understands, especially in her story at the mental asylum, that in her past she may have been hallucinating. In this fantasy, she thinks that Jack Tromm, her first husband, killed her son, that she killed Jack, and that Jack rigged the marriage of Reilly, her former lover, to someone else (*TW*, 211). Later, however, she becomes more open-minded and compassionate. Also she does not behave contradictorily to her true self (*TW*, 210, 211). She merely finds out in the "refuge of the asylum" (*TW*, 211) that she could have been wrong beyond a reasonable doubt about how she thought of Jack and herself. Her hate resulted from her hallucinating about how evil her husband, Jack, and she were. Isa eventually leaves room for change. She realizes she could be wrong about how she thought and lived in the past, and she forgives herself for thinking so negatively about Jack and herself (*TW*, 211, 212).

In a similar manner, Paolo undergoes much suffering before he reconciles himself. Paul, in turn, forgives Isa and looks at her and Jack with compassion (*TW*, 213) for probably the first time in the novel. He finally demonstrates an unconditional love of Isa that was characteristic of the love that came to him from his mother; his sister, Annina; his father; and eventually Isa, his wife. Therefore, Paolo "accepts [Isa] as she was" (*TW*, 213). In time, Paolo realizes he cannot possess/own another soul. This realization was the journey Isa and he had to take "alone": it was a life where certain roads had to be traveled by oneself (*TW*, 213). Isa ultimately becomes, as part of the resolution, symbolically a separate "planet" (*TW*, 214). DiDonato may be saying here that people do not have the right to think that they can control the universe, all planets, and the stars, and ultimately other people's lives, as Paul thought he could. Fortunately, Paul becomes less selfish at the end of the novel than at the beginning, where he tried to control Isa's life.

But before a change, a catharsis, or a cleansing of the characters takes place, we need to look at what both Isa and Paul thought they had done wrong. To understand Isa, a girl from a family of the "Old South" (*TW*, 33), we must understand some of her background. She was a dancer in a theater, and she traveled across the country, where she often had sexual relationships with many men, the first being with her press agent in Nebraska when she was sixteen. In Los Angeles, she meets an older hotel manager, Jack Tromm, and he finally marries her (*TW*, 145). They both leave Los Angeles to live in Modern City. From the beginning, Isa maintains she loved Jack (*TW*, 48). Also, she has relationships with other men, like Jay Monks and Reilly. Much of her past is revealed to us as she talks to Paolo, or in her mind, as she has sex with Paolo. Likewise, Paolo reveals his past in a similar manner, as will be discussed later. In any event, we have these opportunities to view these personal vignettes of thought and speech while the novel unfolds.

First, Isa's "sin" is primarily a trinity involving the feelings of guilt, anger and a loss of self-identity. She, as mentioned previously, believes that her first husband, Jack Tromm, killed her son, and that she should have married Jack Reilly and divorced Jack Tromm. She also feels indirectly responsible for her four-year-old brother's death (*TW*, 207) when she was six. "Her father accused her of the neglect that led to Alexander's [her brother's] death" (*TW*, 207). Just when her father and mother were about to separate, her father went to war and was killed on Armistice Day (*TW*, 207, 208), so Isa felt abandoned and guilty. Her mother, because she felt Isa failed to care for her husband, accused her of killing him when he came home drunk, caught fever, and died (*TW*, 54–55). Before and after Paul marries Isa, he becomes obsessed with Jack Tromm's presence and becomes angry at Isa for mentioning him; he also becomes upset about the remaining memorabilia of Jack Tromm; for instance, her pictures of him (*TW*, 123, 124, 157, 176). Because of these feelings, Isa thinks less of herself than she should.

Second, Paolo's sin is complex; it is one of selfishness and egocentrism that appears mandated as an "original sin" and that also appears to initially lead to doom and to the chaos of the irreconcilability of life. The roots of his sin lie in his past. Like Isa, while making love, he recalls silently within his mind or in discussion with Isa, his first sexual experience with a married woman, Stella L'Africana (*TW*, 35–39; see also *Three Circles of Light*). He also muses over the first sexual intercourse he has with another married woman, Rose O'Malley, when he was eighteen. Like Biff in Arthur Miller's *The Death of a Salesman*, Paolo finds his father in bed with another woman, his American "godmother," Diane Dunn. Suspecting her husband's adulterous affair, "his mother [Paul's Italian mother, Annunziata] sends him to trail his father" (*TW*, 37). His father, after being caught with Diane, then lays the seed for the curse of Paolo's "original sin": "There [are] men's ways [Paolo's father's adulterous ways] and as soon as he [Paolo] [becomes] a man [you] will also understand the way of man" (*TW*, 37). Paolo, however, was to go on feeling even more guilty in his early sexual escapades as he remembered his compassionate, religious mother, Annunziata saying to his sister, "[Mr. O'Malley's] wife [Rose O'Malley] is a whore. I feared she'd get Paolo itching for his first taste of woman. Her breed, the gate opens wide just for a bottle [of wine]" (*TW*, 11). Later, in a dream, Paolo's mother chastises him for "giving love to one used and condemned [to Isa Tromm, a widow]" (*TW*, 182).

So Paul is torn between two sets of standards of behavior, his promiscuous father's and his pure Catholic mother's. Paolo feels doomed to do what his father did and yet felt guilty for these acts, for his pure mother was constantly in his mind. His sister, Annina, also becomes connected with the purity of Annunziata, their mother, adding to Paolo's burden of guilt, mentioned later in the novel. One of Paolo's early sins is expressed by Paul as he recalls his first sexual experience with Stella Africana, who also appears in *Three Circles of Light*:

> Through the Fall and Winter, after school and church, he went to Stella's bed. He took her to his lips and she took him to her lips. He told her that as soon as he was old enough they would get married, be together always. That was the Spring his father was killed in a construction accident. His father's death was the destroying of his Paradise. The Christian God vanquished the pagan God. Imagination wavered. In him the sense of sin and fear were born. His father's death was the wages of sin. His father had been unfaithful to his mother. Stella had betrayed her husband. He had taken Stella's lust to his lips and had

sinned against God and his mother. He had been cursed. His father had lain with his godmother, Diane Dunn. Her baptism of him was the original curse. That was long ago. And since his man years he had easily had eager lust from married women. (*TW*, 39)

Needless to say, Paolo never did get to marry Stella. With this "original sin," Paolo had become Old Adam. Two lies figure prominently in understanding Paolo. "The first conscious lie to his mother" (*TW*, 11) was to tell her on a rainy day when he did not want to lay bricks that he was going to get tools; instead, he commits the sin of adultery with Rose O'Malley. With this first lie, Paul's drive to have sex with a married women is greater than the influence of his own good mother. Thus we can sense Paolo's overriding guilt in the passage above and throughout the novel. The second lie is essential to the understanding of the novel, for the resolution of this lie is connected to the relationship between Isa and Paolo, which is central to the novel. This lie is a lie of "I-communion" (*TW*, 215), a destructive egocentrism within Paul. Paul feels that no other love relationship in Isa's life could have been meaningful except his and that Isa could love only one person, himself. This lie was to cause so much pain to Isa that it would drive her to an insane asylum and almost ruin Paolo completely. Though Paolo's admission of the lie comes as he later reconciles his previous life with Isa, it still provides an insight into how he changed his life for the better, which will be explained more thoroughly later.

> He had romantically, idealistically insisted upon lying to himself that she had not participated in fulsome lust until he came into her, and that with Tromm her giving had been a non-feeling charity and fused obligation; that the institutional life with her first husband had been a quilted covert without care, an unconscious order awaiting his [Paolo's] own advent; that he, her new young husband had been the glorious shock of awakening to her ordained image. (*TW*, 215)

The burden of Paolo's father's sin, sinning with married women, and the betraying of his wife, Annunziata, weighs heavily on Paul in other incidents. As Paulo is having sex with Isa, he hears his father urging him to sin: "Thou art the seed of Geremio whom the American women sought. Do as I did: ram her, devour her, pleasure-death her, and seek not forgiving" (*TW*, 39). In another instance, after his sister's death, he seems to be bent on self-destruction, debauchery, all in a bacchanal to forget the injustice of his sister's death. He also levels this anger about his sister's death at Isa Tromm:

> I'm no good. . . . The day she died I couldn't fall on my knees in church like a man and Christian. I went into the street, a raging animal, picking up women—prostitutes, niggers, schoolgirls, anything!—hotels, drinking, just as I'm doing tonight—three whores before nightfall—and when I raced back to Long Island late at night I went to Christiana . . . now what do you think of that, Mrs. Tromm! (*TW*, 86–87)

Paolo also becomes physically violent with Isa (*TW*, 168). Like Isa's mother, he also accuses Isa of killing her husband (*TW*, 169).

Until Paolo respects the identity of Isa as a woman, no reconciliation or resolution can occur in this novel because Paolo must eliminate his abuse of Isa, his hallucination of reality, especially his obsessiveness about the relationship between Isa and Jack Tromm. He also must eliminate his "original sin" of being bound to the past of his father's sin which perpetuates further self-destruction. "His father's death was the wages of sin" (*TW*, 39). Paolo's treatment of and requests from Isa indicate his jealousy, egocentricity, irrationality and possessiveness. "Before I [Paolo] marry you, these words must come out of your [Isa's] mouth":

> I am glad my husband [Jack Tromm] died. I abhor his life and am happy for his death. I detest myself for having laid with him. I obliterate his identity in this world and the next. If he were alive I would wish him dead both physically and spiritually so that I could truly give myself to you! (*TW*, 124)

Paul's angry attitude toward Isa is to continue manifesting itself even after their marriage.

Just how the resolution of the novel could take place at this point seems unimaginable. However, DiDonato uses extremely creative incidents, reminiscent of episodes in William Faulkner's novels, especially when the coffin slips off the wagon and into the river in *As I Lay Dying*. DiDonato, instead, uses a cemetery scene wherein he actually exhumes and destroys with an ax the corpse of Jack Tromm! Later the insane asylum that Isa enters, after the cemetery scene, plays a vital role in the novel. After Paolo's first visit to the cemetery, he returns home and brings Isa back to the cemetery to further destroy the corpse of Jack Tromm. These imaginative, marvelous, but grim trips to the "underworld" of cemetery and insane asylum, the land of the physically and emotionally/spiritually dead, are instrumental in changing both Isa and Paolo and in resolving the novel. The author now will try to show what happened at the cemetery and the insane asylum and then show how Isa and Paolo thereafter changed or grew, creating a resolution in the novel.

Before this resolution can occur, Paul's "soul had to excavate Jack Tromm from the belly and loins of his wife" (*TW*, 188). He had to destroy Isa's husband "within the Three Circles Of Light," a purgation of the Soul and Mind. (*TW*, 193). But in attempting to excavate Jack Tromm in the cemetery scene, Paolo nearly went insane (*TW*, 168), and certainly Isa did because of his obsessive possessiveness which came about because Paul could not forget that Isa was first married to Jack Tromm (*TW*, 195, 196). Paul's second lie to himself, the selfish egocentric lie that *only he* could be loved by a widow, was to drive him to Jack Tromm's grave in the cemetery scene. The violence and the grimness of this scene indicate Paolo's self-hate as well as his hate for Jack and Isa Tromm. Paul would have to bury this hate to grow as a person. Unfortunately, he does not bury it at this point of the novel.

> He drove to the Skittara Cemetery. In the moonlight he traced Tromm's grave. This [trip] had to be. . . . This grave was [Isa's] brain, and he striking into it with new sacrificial steel. . . . He sweated liberatingly, and glorious youth of itself surged through the spade. The advent of freedom, the strangeness of his deed, illumined his brain and spirit. The metal ping of the spade on the wooden outer casket charged him. (*TW*, 188–89)

Then he thought of Isa and "he clove and splintered the polished coffin" (*TW*, 189). This is reminiscent of the insanity of Markheim in Robert Louis Stevenson's "Markheim" and of Raskolnikov in Dostoyevsky's *Crime and Punishment*. "From the corpse arose a nostril-scraping mousy saccharine stench. . . . He turned on his flashlight. . . . He slashed the aproned funeral suit from the corpse" (*TW*, 192).

In the destruction of Jack's corpse and coffin, Paolo feels an "unbinding from this woman [Isa]" (*TW*, 194). After this initial destruction, Paolo, with his "earthsmeared shoes and clothes and arms" (*TW*, 194), returns home to bring Isa back to the grave site, where she eventually goes insane (*TW*, 195). With Paolo, very docilely, she goes to the grave: "Yes, Paolo. I will do what you want" (*TW*, 194). When they arrive at the grave, anxiously wanting to tell crazed Paolo something,

Isa replies, "I know. I know!" (*TW*, 195). Then Paolo "picked from the earth the dead's withered right hand, put it in her hand and closed her fingers over it. She dropped it. She whispered," as if to pacify Paolo: "When you're through with the garden, I have thrilling news! Hurry, dear, hurry" (*TW*, 195). After returning to the car, she attempts to give Paolo an explanation (*TW*, 195) of a secret she promised to tell him previously during the cemetery scene but never did (*TW*, 186–87). At the cemetery, her happiness is almost an insane, but optimistic, sort of happiness which actually ironically foreshadows the somewhat reconciliatory outcome of the novel:

> "It is happening to us, taking place right now, it is wonderful, wonderful beyond words." She pointed to the stars. "That's part of it. They are dead, watching. We have to be very careful. Darling, we have been chosen. I don't want you to be upset about anything. There is nothing but you and me and the hidden power who is guarding our every movement. It is all planned. There is nothing that can hurt us now. I have the answer [to the secret mentioned on 187], the answer has come to me; all will be wonderful as it is meant to be; the mysterious secrets fit together perfectly." (*TW*, 195)

As day breaks, "from her draining sanity" (*TW*, 195), she is cut off from her statement, and we, as readers, now enter with her the insane asylum she is committed to, "The Answer . . . is . . ." (*TW*, 195). In a quick change of scene, Paolo is sitting by her at the insane asylum. The destruction of the coffin and corpse in the cemetery is actually the first agonizing step toward Isa's and Paolo's search for self and each other, rending from each of their lives, though violently, that which in them is restraining them from growth. Paul must eliminate his obsession with the Tromms; Isa must learn to assert her own identity, both to herself, to Paolo, and to the world.

This identity that Isa must discover takes place in two stages: earlier in the novel, at the mental asylum where she recognizes and identifies her problems; and, ultimately, at the end of the novel, at the beach, where Paolo recalls how she solves her problem (*TW*, 212). In the first stage, Isa recalls her guilt and hate connected with the trinity of her sin, previously mentioned; she thought that Jack Tromm had killed her first son, that she had killed her first husband, and that she had failed to marry Reilly and divorce Jack Tromm (*TW*, 202–11). She also recalls with guilt the death of her own brother (*TW*, 207). In addition, she cannot forget her promiscuous past (*TW*, 208, 209, 210). Indeed, "she had descended into the underworld for her dead husband and her live husband. She had come back by herself" (*TW*, 202). In the second stage, Isa asserts her identity by forgiving herself and others. She eliminates her past guilt by reshaping the thinking of her past into a more positive direction:

> She wondered about Jack's role in the loss of her first child—had it just been emotional suspicion on her part? Suppose it were true; the child was not a person who had lived and whom she had seen and known; Jack loved her to the point that she had seen and known; Jack loved her to the point that he could not share her affection even with children, and what more attention could a woman wish for. She admitted to herself at last that the manner of Jack's death . . . was a fluke, one of those things. . . . The day of Reilly's wedding was a crazy wild one; she and Jack were heavily drunk and how could it count what they were saying and doing. . . . Jack, for the first time in their long marriage . . . , became temporarily suicidal, opened the windows, shut off the steam, passed out before he could come to his senses. (*TW*, 211)

In addition, Isa solves her problem of Paolo's abuse of her by being assertive again:

> You tried to make yourself my God and have me confess to you. This is America. Your God and mine are strangers. I have nothing to confess. Your unfair God and all your other elements can go get lost. You're in the wrong world. My world is the world of my own experience. No one but I have lived my life for me. I am not afraid to live or afraid to die. Whether you like it or not I'll tell you what you can't take: the truth. The few men in my life did not take me; I knew what I was doing; I wanted them, just like I wanted you; it's too late in the day to lie. (*TW*, 212)

Isa also seems to find her "identity" (*TW*, 200) when she discovers she is pregnant (*TW*, 200) at the asylum. Isa then states she will agree to bring Paolo's son, as well as another of his sons, into the world (*TW*, 212–13). "Beyond that" she "promises nothing" (*TW*, 213). Paolo will recall these words in a positive fashion as he later plays with his children on the beach (*TW*, 212), what I consider as part of the resolution of the novel that occurs on the last page of the book (*TW*, 222). The "albatross" around Isa's neck is then cut off in the asylum, for there she finds her own identity. She had seen "Pluto" (*TW*, 201), and, in "sleeping in deepest dreamless sleep for days without interruption, . . . an imitation of death" (*TW*, 201) she, starting to find herself, becomes "fascinated . . . for the first time" with her face (*TW*, 201). Finally, in a therapeutic statement of self-discovery, she says, "I am not Isa Tromm. I am not Isa di Alba. I am Isa Latham [her maiden name], stronger than any weak bastard of a man I screw with. Isa Latham will survive and live!" (*TW*, 201).

Paolo's growth is related to his undoing of his two lies, mentioned previously, the first having to do with breaking the bond of his own father's sin "to have eager lust with married women" (*TW*, 39); instead he will follow the command of his pure mother to have children and raise a family (*CC*, 310–11). Paolo's egocentric lie has to do with eliminating the falsehood that Isa could not have loved her first husband, Jack Tromm; selfishly, Paolo thought he only was meant to be loved by Isa. He felt Isa could not and should not have loved anyone else. The events that change Paolo are the cemetery scene and the breakdown of Isa and her commitment to the insane asylum.

First, Paolo's second lie will be discussed. Upon his visit to the asylum, when Paolo realizes that he has driven Isa insane, he begins to become less egocentric:

> But the permanent abode of his Soul had been apprised of the lie from the beginning, and rejected it. Again, as before, that which suckled her [Isa's] substance and evolved in her belly would be more than hers and his; a life his Soul had called for to be of God's children, and with its very own Sacred Soul awaiting it. (*TW*, 215)

When Paolo first sees Isa the day after the cemetery scene, he also realizes how he has contributed to his wife's breakdown: "Isa, I love you. Isa, what has my love done to you! . . ." (*TW*, 195). While contrasting Isa's state to his, Paolo continues to feel a purifying guilt, rather than the hopelessly destructive guilt he previously experienced: "You [Paolo] could see he [Paolo] felt irretrievable, guilty for being sane" (*TW*, 197). After Isa's experience in the insane asylum, Paolo takes a trip to Florida with his wife and child. It is here that Paolo has time to think of his past, and a good deal of reconciliation occurs here as he recalls how Isa assertively told him she could have truly loved Jack, her first husband, and that she would try to pick up the pieces of Paul's marriage and bear two sons for him. We, as readers, see that the road to growth, as Paolo said earlier, is an inner journey (*TW*, 213, 215), as well as one taken with other people. Paul begins to have compassion for his wife and Jack Tromm:

> This woman was the same as many women; a woman necessary, as the earth is to the swirling seed and the sower's hand. The balm of peace transcending came to him and removed him from her, and with it lightened the burden of his need of her. From his entablature he could look *unselfishly* down upon this Isa and Tromm *with sympathy* as if viewing from an elevated detachment their mutuality of common equilibrium, and her deprivation and vacuity of the same by his death. (*TW*, 213; italics mine)

This death to self is what kills Paolo's second lie, the hate he has for Isa and Jack Tromm that resulted from his egocentric thinking that allowed him to believe he could win, control and possess another person, another woman, Isa Tromm.

Next, the antithesis of Paolo's first lie is honesty. In the presence of home, hearth, family, Paolo's lust is controlled: "There could not be another Isa for him, the madness could not be repeated, and through her he had come to love women more dearly" (*TW*, 217), rather than without respect as he had done for a good part of his life. By being present at his wife's childbirth, Paolo becomes more of a man: "And he looked to himself as man. And she loved him for his deep-deep love of her son. His morbid Paul-self was departing" (*TW*, 216). The "purification" of Paolo in this scene of childbirth is a step in fulfilling Annunziata's and Annina's [his sister's] wish of purity and the happiness of having a family: "He kissed Isa's forehead as he had done to his mother and sister, and there was the first spilling of the cleansing, pure waters upon him and her" (*TW*, 216). At this juncture, a "baptism" of maturity occurs for Paolo. This identity and growth is directly proportional to his love for Isa and his new son. As the novel approaches its end, Paolo continues to grow.

The ending of the novel is a moving scene. Although the road to identity for Paul will not be easy in his future, it is my belief that the novel is very optimistic, convincing and reconciliatory at its end. As Paul sits with his family on the beach in Florida, his thoughts are temporarily pulled to the sins of "lust" in the form of a tempting "mythological Lucinda," who appears in his mind (*TW*, 219). But then we are "awakened" by Isa shouting at a dazed husband, "Wake up and live! Look! Your son, Paul, wants to walk by himself. God bless him" (*TW*, 220). Annunziata's prediction at the end of *Christ in Concrete* (*CC*, 310-311) is fulfilled here in *This Woman*.

I believe that *This Woman* is the key to the corpus of DiDonato's fiction and drama. In *This Woman* Paul will be blessed with children and "home" (*TW*, 220). To come "home" is to find one's identity (*TW*, 30, 159, 160, 170, 217, 220). Even in DiDonato's first novel, *Christ in Concrete*, Paul's dream is to bring an "ashamed stranger who betrayed Annunziata" (295) back "home." This "stranger" is, of course, Paul's father. To return home is to forgive and to be beloved. In DiDonato's play, *The Love of Annunziata*, in Annunziata's mind, Geremio, Paul's father, comes home and dances the tarantella with Annunziata; Annunziata has forgiven and loved Geremio. She truly has accepted him. As was said at the beginning of this chapter, the author does not agree with Bauer's statement that the novel is contradictory and that it is not convincing;[7] he disagrees with Rose Basile Green who says the novel is "disturbing" and "unbalanced."[8] He feels the reason these comments were made may have been because the novel is a psychologically complex novel about two people who have been through the agony of the underworld. Despite this difficult journey, both Paul and Isa see vestiges of Paradise. Paul frees himself of the primitive, mythological "Lucinda" and runs to his child and wife on the beach. Paul, indeed, is back in reality:

> A vaulting apocalypse illuminated him. His [Paolo's] immediate pagan satyr mortal, and Catholic Soul eternal dashed into close, secret embrace.
>
> He arose, ran to Isa and their child, clasped to him the hearth and sacred fire. (*TW*, 220)

That final "clasp" of his wife and child is the clasp of Annunziata and Annina. Both Annunziata and Annina represent an order and beauty indicated in the novel by the "stars and planets" (*TW*, 32, 38, 57, 71, 192, 195, 214). This purity, order, beauty, sincerity as well as religiosity of Annunziata and Annina triumph in this novel, as opposed to the world of theater (*TW*, 58, 83, 160, 179, 214, 218, 319),[9] which represents emotionalism, pretension, and acting in the most negative sense of these words.

Paolo, at the end of the novel, answers a question he asked at an earlier tumultuous stage of his life: "Is there no exit from this theatre [absurdity of life]?" (*TW*, 21). The absurdity of life is also referred to at another point as a "prostitute" (*TW*, 176). At the end of the novel, Paul has managed to shake off the sin of his ancestors, especially his father's ("the pagan satyr mortal," *TW*, 220), the conscious sense of sin or "the sense of sin and fear of God" (*TCOL*, 246) and to embrace the "Catholic

Soul" (*TW*, 220), (the purity of family, love, order, represented by Annunziata and Annina and their religious fervor). This "affirmation" in the novel has indeed finally come but at great expense. The Old Adam in Paolo embraces and takes on a New Adam (*TW*, 30). Isa's bittersweet prediction, her secret, comes closer to reality at the end of the novel: "All will be wonderful as it is meant to be; the mysterious secrets fit together perfectly" (*TW*, 195). *This Woman* is an imaginative, deep, meaningful novel; by no means is it a "sexual potboiler," as Michael Esposito contends.[10] "The flowering of womanhood" that Annunziata mentions in *Christ in Concrete* (311) becomes the "flowering of deathing" that Isa and Paul experience in *This Woman* (214). In a nightmare Paul has in *Christ in Concrete*, he sees his father, who says to him: "Not even the Death can free us, for we are . . . Christ in concrete . . ." (*CC*, 298). The author sees *This Woman* as exemplifying a triumph over this statement, for Paul and Isa begin to live at the end of the novel—they are freed spiritually. This freedom is also illustrated in another passage in *Christ in Concrete* after Paul and his mother have returned from the seer, Mrs. Nicholls. A consciousness tells Paul's family while they pray, "The living do not die" (*CC*, 158). Paul's dream/nightmare exhortation in *Christ in Concrete* to his father, "Refuse to die" (298) becomes a reality fulfilled in *This Woman*. Indeed, Isa and Paul come alive in *This Woman*. DiDonato answered Dorothee von Huene-Greenberg's question about whether we would be buried in concrete with the words, "Yes, fate gets you, see," yet he also answered his art in his "reprisal" where he can "see light."[11] DiDonato said his art is like "the only opening where [he could] breathe, the opening where [he could] see light. . . . It's my only defense."[12] This art was related "to transfiguring humanity into a brotherhood, into a paradise."[13] *This Woman*, therefore, is a "reprisal" of "light;" it sees light, in the author's opinion. *This Woman* is an agonizing search for woman, for a man's wife, but it is also that same search that finds the spirit and love of Paul's own mother, Annunziata, and his sister, Annina. The light of the "hearth" (*TW*, 220) and the "sacred fire" (*TW*, 220) of "home" in the context of nature's beach and sea, like the optimistic dream of Paul's godfather, Nazone, in *Christ in Concrete* (280–83), will light up the "kingdom of the night" of the "behorned satyr" of *Three Circles of Light* (246). In the novel *Three Circles of Light*, Annunziata says Geremio, Paul's father, is building a "home" (244) in heaven. She says this house will not be complete until her children are men and women with children of their own and she is old and until they "ceaselessly pray" (*TCOL*, 244). Paul arrives at this stage in *This Woman*!

The compromise of life involves an acceptance of both sadness and joy.[14] That prayerlike wish of that young boy worker about to be an adult, Paul in *Christ in Concrete,* is fulfilled in *This Woman*; a "resurrection" of life occurs: "O mother, home I come with father's hands. . . . Mother, lift your heart and rejoice for father is in Heaven and we shall rise" (*CC,* 104). Paul of *This Woman* has seen death, and he has come alive! Paul's unrealized desire to be whole at the end of *Three Circles* is finally realized in *This Woman,* for he has replaced hate with some semblance of reason and acceptance: "Reason being removed from love as the earth from the stars, we [the Geremio family] sought in vain the image of Father" (*TCOL,* 241). Paul has found his father in *This Woman* by being more reasonable in his life. He truly has also found a Mother, the female component, as well as a Father, a male component.[15] Isa, his wife, also finds herself. *This Woman* is, therefore, central to the corpus of DiDonato's literature, especially his longer fiction and drama.

8
Christ in Concrete

In contrasting Ben Barzman's and Edward Dmytryk's versions of Pietro DiDonato's novel, *Christ in Concrete*, Harry M. Geduld, in his 1984–85 article, characterizes the novel as "peopled with wooden characterizations, and rather vague as to its message in total import."[1] Geduld feels that the novel's "meaning and purpose" are unclear and vague.[2] I disagree with this statement, as probably would scholars like Michael Esposito, Barbara Gae Bauer, and Rose Basile Green. It is my belief that Pietro DiDonato's first autobiographical novel, published in 1939, is meaningful for several reasons.

First, it is a novel primarily of socioeconomic or political protest as well as a protest of oppression of any kind. Second, it is a novel about love that comes from the human heart. Third, it fulfills a vital function in developing the corpus of DiDonato's work, especially in providing the foundation for tracing the development of Paul, or Paolo.

In order to understand the novel's multiple messages, it would be valuable to examine some of DiDonato's statements made earlier in this study. When asked why he writes, DiDonato said he does so first to tell a "story" with a "message" (*DIOM*, 104). He also said, as has been mentioned before, that love can shame death (*DIOM*, 105). He also mentions the good his Mom and Dad did for their human beings is what matters (*DIOM*, 100–101, 105). He mentioned that life takes place in "mystery" (*DIOM*, 104–5) and love results from this sacredness (*DIOM*, 105). Not only these comments, but his comments on "victimization" (*DIOM*, 99–103) and his search for "justice" and sense of being a "protester" (*DIOM*, 101) with a sense of "rebellion" (*DIOM*, 99–103) are also evident in DiDonato's novel, *Christ in Concrete*. DiDonato also said that *Christ in Concrete* was his purest work (*DIOM*, 102, 113).

These statements of DiDonato are, I feel, intricately bound to the meaning and message of *Christ in Concrete*. In its most general sense, *Christ in Concrete* is a novel depicting the coldness of the world and how it affects an Italian-American family and community, though its universal application is also obvious. But *Christ in Concrete* is much more than this. It is also a triumph of the spirit, of the love that allows one to endure that coldness that is characteristic of injustice and, sometimes, of spiritual death.

Christ in Concrete is also a novel about love that comes from the heart. Warren French calls it a beautiful study of love.[3] Richard Chase, in discussing the characteristics of the novel, quotes Hawthorne as believing that a romance must not "swerve aside from the truth of the human heart."[4] Chase also says that "to keep fiction in touch with the human heart is to give it a universal human significance."[5] William Faulkner, in his 1950 "Nobel Prize Acceptance Speech," mentioned that a writer should write about "the old verities and truths of the heart—love, and honor and pity and pride and compassion and sacrifice."[6] *Christ in Concrete* does not "swerve aside from the truth of the human heart,"[7] Hawthorne's definition of a novel as romance, and it deals with those "old verities and truths of the heart."[8]

This "truth of the human heart"[9] is manifested in the several meaningful messages found in *Christ in Concrete:* its economic, social, political, religious, psychological, and literary themes. To put it simply, I have seen at least three levels of meaning or three messages in *Christ in Concrete*. The first is a literary statement of protest against the coldness of injustice and oppression, largely by those in power, such as those in institutions and bureaucracies. Though the Italian-Americans in the novel experience all of these inequities, the applicability of the novel's universality is quite evident.

The first message of the novel deals with the abuses of injustice: the Church; the "corporation" as represented by the evils of the construction (masonry) business; the government, as represented by any of its agencies, including not only the American government as a whole, but its agencies of the welfare department; workmen's compensation; and the police department. In contrast to focusing on these abusers, the second message is the message of the "truth of the human heart."[10] For the development of this point, I will discuss how two characters in particular demonstrate the "verities of the heart,"[11] though I bring in other applicable characters and ideas.

The third message is a complex one and one that I think Geduld fails to see, possibly because he does not appear to interpret *Christ in Concrete* as playing a meaningful role in the context of DiDonato's corpus of literature. In this corpus we can trace DiDonato's development of the fictional and autobiographical character, Paul, to his fullest development in *This Woman*, the pinnacle of DiDonato's work. The corpus of his other works—*Three Circles of Light*, *The Love of Annunziata*, and "Christ in Plastic"—will be better understood by understanding *Christ in Concrete*. This meaningful role of *Christ in Concrete*, especially the episode of Paul's dream/nightmare (295), in DiDonato's corpus is the third message.

Before the discussion of these three messages begins, the story will be briefly summarized. The story largely centers around chapter 1, "Geremio," the accidental death of Paul's father, which first appeared as a short story in *Esquire*, after taking DiDonato a month to write.[12] Paolo's father, Geremio, a construction foreman/worker, living in Hoboken, dies by falling off a construction scaffold on Good Friday, March 30. Later in the novel, Vincenzo Nazone, Paolo's godfather, while working, also dies by falling off a scaffold on July 28. Paolo dreadfully fears falling as they both did, and his daily journey to Job (going to work) is characterized as a battle or war (15, 87, 103, 117, 147, 188, 189; unless otherwise indicated, page references in this chapter will be to *Christ in Concrete*).[13] After his father's death, Paolo takes over as "father" (49) for his seven brothers and sisters who live with his mother, Annunziata. The rest of the novel covers Paolo's journey as "father."

Before we go on to discuss the several themes of the novel, it should be pointed out that even though DiDonato concentrates on the Italian-American experience, he speaks also about the universality of the human experience which is opposed to injustice. Paul's definition of people is universal at best:

> So different were people, thought Paul in his bedroom darkness. After the show of day, after all the incidents and faces and voices and smells, what was he to think? Did they not all live one atop the other and feel and taste and smell each other? Did not Job [work] claim all? With what all-embracing thought could he bless America today?
>
> They, like me, are children of Christ (CC, 140).[14]

After his father's fall, Paul has a nightmare, after which Dr. Murphy tells him to rest (132). As Paul has time to think, he visualizes, as he looks at "shadows" (135) on the wall, that all humanity has a commonality of experience and existence. Jubilantly, he contemplates workers and members of his community, especially two members, Katarina and the Lucy, and he says,

Or were they the men of Job? They became countless and were all the people of the world.... Here was the answer to everything. He felt like one who was never born and would never die, and as he tried to stay awake, darkness was closing over him. (135–36)

Later, Annunziata, Paul's mother, points out at the Workmen's Compensation State Bureau the universality of all who suffer, especially the poor: "They [the poor] were as herself. They were wounded and sought the helping hand of Christ's Christians" (171–72). To the bureaucratic abusers of the Workmen's Compensation Bureau, Annunziata also shows her dissatisfaction: "They seem not of Christ" (171). And finally, in the shout of a hardworking Maestro Farabutti at the marriage of Cola and Luigi, Farabutti's words describe Italian-Americans, though he echoes words that could also depict the self-value that any person affirms: "We are Italians! Know what that means? It means the regal blood of terrestrial man.... The I-tal-lian-nne is the flower of Christians" (261–62). DiDonato seems to be saying with these incidents that all people's journeys include both pain and joy[15] and the incarnate experience for some enables them to transcend the pain which appears to be fairly universal.[16] From Adam and Eve our die has been cast for work.[17] DiDonato made an interesting parallel for Dorothee von Huene-Greenberg: "Any portrayal of Christianity must always portray the 'have nots,' the workers, the poor who have nothing to lose but their honor and their lives."[18]

Now we may address the first ideational concern or theme of the novel. Here an attempt is made to show how DiDonato makes a statement of protest against the Church. Idealistic, twelve-year-old Paul, after his father's tragic fall, makes a visit to the church to ask that his father be "brought back" (79) from death. Outside of the church, he meets Katarina, a neighborhood friend, who asks him what he was doing in church and who gives him food after he tells her, "There is nothing [to eat] at home" (79). Paul tells Katarina he is certain to get help from Father John (79). Katarina accompanies him to church but does not enter the rectory after an old man working at the rectory rudely puts off Paul. Finally, Paul meets Father John, asks for help and for food, but receives answers from Father John that indicate the insensitivity and non-involvement often characteristic of bureaucracies. In the "high severe chambers" near a "table" containing rich and ample food (81), Father John refers Paul first to Welfare, then to Workmen's Compensation, and then suggests neighbors' help (81–82). While Father John is speaking, Paul, in his mind, keeps wondering about the table with all the food on it, and wonders who eats all that food—no doubt his seven brothers and sisters and mother are in his mind (81). Finally, two of Father John's statements and other incidents fracture Paul's idealistic thinking about the church and later infuriate Katarina once he exits the rectory and tells her what happened. First, Father John gives him the cold answer: "I have nothing to do with charities. There is a board of trustees who confer and pass on every expenditure. Do you understand?" (83). Next, Father John gives Paul a portion of "strawberry shortcake" (83) to bring to his hungry family. The last incident, though not as cruel, reminds one of the famous line of Marie Antoinette that denigrates the poor in Charles Dickens' *A Tale of Two Cities*, "Let them eat cake." Paul felt he needed immediate, long-term, significant help, but he was obviously not getting it from the church.

The second statement of oppression comes in the scene at the police station shortly after Paul's father's death. In answer to Paul's request for information on the building's collapse, the policeman responds, "Oh, yeah, the wop [Geremio, Paul's father] is under the wrappin' paper out in the courtyard" (40). Later, in search of food, Paul again stops at the police station and contemplates going in, but hesitates and never enters when he hears the voice of the same policeman he heard before and his repeated phrase about the "wop" under the "wrappin' paper" (77).

Before the ways in which the government, its representatives, or power structures symbolize injustice are explained, we will examine a demonstration of protest, not only against America and all governments, but especially against the Russian government, that is made by means of allusions to Paul's Russian Jewish friend, Louis Molov, and his family. These allusions more or less point out injustices in the world. To Paul, the Russian Jewish family living in the tenement "smelled of earth" (164). Louis tells Paul that his brother, Leov, "a brilliant poet" and "student" who "loved everyone" (165), was killed during the World War by the Russian czar, for "organizing the peasants against the war" (165). Leov "hated money and war and cruel people" (165). Louis also tells of further oppression: "Every day people died about us. Starved. Killed. They were workers and peasants. Families were cut to pieces by the Czar's sharp swords" (168).[19] It is important to mention here that DiDonato has admitted sympathies he holds for the common man and justice (*CIP*).[20]

Another incident concerning the Jewish family reflects the injustice of war and its killing of martyred soldiers. Annunziata, Paul, and Louis Molov go to the cemetery on Memorial Day. They view Geremio's tombstone as Paul and Louis make a promise to return on every Memorial Day to "think of [Paul's] father and [Louis'] brother, Leov." Paul also contemplates other American soldiers who have died: "He saw the armies of seeking faces in corridors and the endlessly bending figures of his dreams" (184). All the incidents concerning the Jewish family describe them as trying to express their ideals. In these incidents, war or some other injustice plays a part in bringing the involved characters to their deaths. DiDonato's own sympathies with idealists, visionaries and even revolutionaries for justice are quite well documented.[21] His aversion to war is substantiated by his biography, since he was "a conscientious objector in World War II."[22] His respect for the Jewish immigrants as a peaceful group has also been noted.[23]

Continuing the discussion of incidents concerning Louis Molov, there is, in the author's opinion, another interesting parallel to note about the treatment of humans. As both Paul and Louis sit at a waterfront, Louis tells a sad story about seeing his two friends drown in Russia. This serious story, the author believes, is parallel to the story of Paul's friends who swim naked and then later surround Gloria Olson on a dock as she tries to escape them (110). "Paul felt ashamed for her" (160). "He [Paul] was older than all those children of his own age" (160). One is led to think that the juxtaposition of these two stories in two separate incidents in the novel points out the seeming cruelty of life, one created by the fates of gods and one by the insensibility of young boys—Paul is shocked that Louis cannot believe in God after Louis tells the story of his brother (185). In any event, our appreciation of a Christ figure, one who is treated "unjustly," is more understandable after these two scenes. The first scene of seriousness and empathy with which Louis Molov tells his story is contrasted to the cruel, insensitive behavior of the boys on a dock.

The cold treatment received at two other government offices, the Welfare and Workmen's Compensation Bureau, is oppressing. Ironically, the building Paul walks into after his father's death has the words "Justice" and "Equality" on the stone over its entrance (75). It is to the "Overseer of the Poor, Room 302" (75) that Paul walks. He then receives inconsiderate answers to his questions about the building collapse that killed his father, as the following interchange indicates.

> "What building collapse? Never heard about it. Was he an American citizen?"
> "He had taken out his first papers."
> "But he's dead."
> "Yes . . ."
> "Well, then, he wasn't a citizen." (75)

Also, when Annunziata enters the Workmen's Compensation State Bureau and tries to recover money for her husband's fall, she compassionately views the people needing help there as being "wounded and seeking the helping hand of Christ" (171). Becoming very angry at these injustices, in her mind she negatively characterizes the unconcerned, cold workers:

> What do they here? They look not anguished and tightly pressed. They look not humble and at sea. They look not part of grief, and seem masters. They bear transparent distant eye of policeman. They seem not of Christ. (171)

Annunziata was correct in sizing up the Workmen's Compensation State Bureau, for Geremio's compensation case proves unsuccessful (176). The biased statements from boss Murdin that the cause of the collapse was attributable to "Eyetalian laborers" (174) not being able to supervise themselves and getting themselves into all kinds of trouble reveals the injustice of the whole case hearing (171–72). Murdin makes derogatory statements about the workers' "confusing" names (173–74) when asked who was foreman on the job; Murdin never admits Geremio was foreman, and he downgrades Geremio's position as laborer (173). Murdin never admits the causes of the collapse, which were construction safety infractions which Geremio had unsuccessfully attempted to correct (18, 21, 24, 25). Later, in a nightmare/dream, it is no wonder that Paul visualizes Mr. Murdin as the representative of the cold, unfair bureaucracy or colder institutionalized power: "He has a suit and mask of a general, a mayor, a principal, a policeman" (296).

In DiDonato's interview with the author, he mentioned the insensitivity of "victimization" (*DIOM*, 99–103). The guilt that often occurs in victims, especially Italian-American immigrants, could be compared to our American puritanical guilt. This feeling of guilt is seen in Hawthorne's work. It can be sensed in the following passage that appears after the unfortunate, unsuccessful Compensation Board hearing:

> That night was passed ... in the feeling that for *some* reason the family of Geremio was wrong, ... that the men who sweated and cursed on Job were wrong, that they were cheap, immoral, a weight of charity and wrong to the mysterious winning forces of right. (177–78)

In sensing the ill treatment of the Italian-American immigrant and community, Paul then thinks, "O God above, what world and country are we in? We didn't mean to be wrong" (178). Finally the chapter "Job" and the compensation case echo that sense of Italian-American guilt or American puritanical guilt: "Born in sin said the walls. Born in sin said the dark. Born in sin said the air. Born in sin said fear" (178). When the author reads DiDonato or talks with him, he can better understand the psychology of thinking of the victim (*DIOM*, 99–103). The abuser corrupts a person's self-image so much that the victim can be incapacitated to act (*DIOM*, 99–103).

The "corporation" is the next oppressor in the novel (101, 107, 110, 116, 119, 126–29, 130–31, 183, 287, 289). The "corporation" is the employer or the construction (masonry) business. It creates the low paying and poor working conditions of Job (work) which Paul and the Paesanos face as a war or battle (15, 87, 103, 107, 117, 187, 189). One of the most gruesome displays of cold treatment toward the worker as a human comes after Nazone's fall to death. The impersonal order of the superintendent to immediately return the laborers to work emphasizes the profit motive, rather than a concern for the worker as a person: "Boys . . . there's a lotta mortar in the mixer and tubs that's gotta be used up. There's a hundred brickies and sixty hod carriers and overhead" (289). In addition, Paul, since he is young, is underpaid five dollars by Rinaldi, the foreman of the "corporation" (129–30). Rinaldi's cold response to Paul's question about the unfairness of the payment is, "That's the way the world is" (130–31). Shortly after this incident, Paul has a nightmare in which he feels he cannot pay the bills of the family (131–32). This nightmare is also significant, for Paul feels his heart will "explode" (132). Shortly after, Dr. Murphy suggests that Paul not work for awhile because of his "strained heart" (132). As a foil to the corporation's treatment of the workers, DiDonato creates the character of Dr. Murphy who charges nothing for his bill (132). Certainly, Dr. Murphy's function in the novel indicates he is not "a wooden characterization."[24] The "corporation," in this case the construction business, as was mentioned, is inconsiderate of the workers' working conditions (18, 21, 24, 25). Another worker, named the Lucy because he loved an opera with Lucia in it, protests the unequal balance between the profit made by the corporation and the low pay and poor working conditions of the workers: "That's what the America does for your peasants. Vomit your poison, you miserable bastards [fellow workers], for when you go to scratch the louse from your hungry faces you will not even possess the luxury of fingernails" (107). Even some of the workers become part of the corporation when they blame Paul for laying brick without being properly instructed (127).

The second message of *Christ in Concrete* is that it does not "swerve from the truth of the human heart,"[25] and that it is filled with Faulkner's "verities of the truth of the heart."[26] To develop this idea, the author will speak of two loving characters, Nazone, Paul's godfather, and Paul's mother, Annunziata.

It is true that Geremio's fall off the scaffold is often emphasized in the novel, and that it plays an important part, but the place in the novel of Nazone and his fall also should be accentuated. It is the author's thought that Paul was closer to Nazone than most readers realize.

Except for the incident where Paul is shocked at Nazone's "French pictures" (221, 222, 225) and at the fact that Nazone has indulged in sex with a prostitute (221), Nazone is portrayed as being most compassionate, especially to Paul and his family, as well as others. At Luigi's wedding, Nazone, sounding like Lambert Strether in Henry James' novel, *The Ambassadors*, as he says to young Bilham, "Live—all you can,"[27] tells all present, "Come . . . what does one let himself live for if not to enjoy!" (246). After Geremio's death, Paul gets a job as a bricklayer through Nazone's efforts (91–95), even though Rinaldi almost rejects Paul because he weighs only seventy-five pounds (101) and because Paul is only twelve (101). Nazone also helps train Paul for construction work (102, 216). As a result, Paul is so elated with his own work that he utters lines reminiscent of the optimistic outcome of DiDonato's other novel, *This Woman*. In short, this resurrected, happy and self-accepting utterance brings Paul out of the valley of death, the fear that he cannot find work: "O mother, home I come with father's hands. . . . Mother, lift your heart and rejoice, for Father is in Heaven and we shall rise!" (104). And then because of Nazone's assistance, Paul develops a sense of courage and identity, both displayed here and foreshadowing Paul's later development in *This Woman*: "Mama—nothing can happen to me—" (*CC*, 105). This line is probably the most optimistic line in the novel or in the whole corpus of DiDonato's work. It is no wonder, then, that Hunt-Hunt, another worker, characterizes Nazone as a caring person: "Nazone . . . has a warm little heart beating under his arm" (94). When Paul is underpaid, Nazone buys Paul clothes (112), promises Paul's marriage to his daughter in Abruzzi (112, 211), and inspires Paul after his father's death: "Courage, little godson, and faith, and you shall be a great builder" (112). Nazone also helps Paul get work again after he is laid off (279). On Christmas Eve at midnight, the spirit of Nazone's religiosity is humorously made fun of. The workers, after some drinking and loose sexual play with some Polish girls, "crucify" Nazone (209–13). The Lucy "fashions a crown of rope with nails" (212). The workers ask

Nazone to give a religious sermon, where he says, not accidentally in the light of DiDonato's literary work, "Only the good are crucified" (211). This statement is later ironically realized, for he is pushed off a scaffold by an angry foreman (286–88). Like Geremio, Nazone and Paul go to work or to "battle" or "war" every day (15, 87, 103, 117, 187–89). However, before his death, Nazone, possibly sensing he might die at work, tries to convince Paul not to go to work the day he is killed, but instead to go to the beach (279–84).[28] These passages and words are a marvelous epitaph for a compassionate godfather, Nazone. Nazone, sounding like a St. Francis Assisi, tries to convince Paul of the magnificence of the day and of all nature:

> This life of mine is inspired now, right now this very moment, to find itself on the rim splay of sea with one naked foot on warm white sand and the other in ocean's wet green. I don't know, but this day is a canzonella of God, a day lucent with colored glass bells. Madonna, with this mood I have a volition for laughing things like this bright circular sun atop our heads, a lust for things natural! (281)

> We may bless the senses with smell of grass and salt of sea. (281)

However, Paul, concerned about the loss of a day's pay (281), joins Nazone, and they instead go to work, where Nazone is finally shoved off the platform after Foreman Jones' "mad foot catches the tub" (285) and "throws" (285) Paul into Nazone, sending Nazone to his fall. Shortly before this fall, Nazone was thinking of the "coves" and "dunes" of his native Abruzzi (285) and of "earth" and "sea" (285). It is no wonder that Paul has a nightmare of Nazone after the fall (293). In fact, Paul hears Nazone say in this nightmare, "Paul will seek Christ[,] he will seek Christ for that is his mission, . . . He now will find Him" (294).[29] Nazone, unlike the cold bureaucracies, is not "dead," for he loves and cares for others. His heart is not dead. It is the author's opinion that he has for the most part a very positive influence on Paul.

Another person who loves and cares for others is Annunziata, Paul's mother. Though Paul's mother expels Paul from his home when he crushes her cross (304), when he calls the crucifix a "lie" (302), when he denies the power of God to resurrect his papa (303) and when he feels that "justice" (304) or "salvation" (307) is not present in the world, she still loves Paul. She later, in her mind, asks for forgiveness: "My Paul—forgive me." "Dio . . . forgive him [Paul]—he knows not of what he says or does . . . " (305–6). Later, when she is dying, Paul returns to ask her forgiveness (307, 310) and Annunziata does absolve him and designates him as the leader of the family:

> Son . . . everything in my world is for thee. For thee I desire the fullest gifts of heaven—To thee must the good Dio bestow the world—and lasting health. He must bless thee with the flower of womankind and many-many children as yourself . . . and joy and peace without measure—for to me—thou art most precious. . . . (310–11)
>
> Children, wonderful . . . love . . . love love . . . love ever our Paul . . . Follow him. (CC, 311)

For Paul, the fulfillment of having children and coming to some sort of resolution with and acceptance of life, though not perfect, will be fulfilled in *This Woman*, as is made evident in the chapter devoted to that work in this book.

Annunziata's vision of seeing the world filled with Christ and love is evident elsewhere in *Christ in Concrete*; as has been said, she senses the non-caring atmosphere of the Workmen's Compensation State Bureau when she thinks to herself, "They [the workers of the Bureau] seem not of Christ" (171). Annunziata's "home" is synonymous with peace for her husband, Geremio, and herself (14). As demonstrated by the author in *This Woman* and *The Love of Annunziata*, "home" is a place where love reigns. DiDonato contrasts Annunziata's peace of home with the alliterative use of the letter "s" in his depiction of the battlefield of the Job, the construction workfield: "The day, like all day*s*, came to an end. Callou*s*ed and brui*s*ed bodie*s s*ighed, and numb leg*s s*huffled towards happy railroad flat*s*" (14, emphasis mine; see also 15, 27, 126). Annunziata's spirit is the epitome of endurance; she closely resembles Christ's mother, Mary of Sorrows, when she wonders about how the family will get food after Geremio's death:

> For the walls who destroyed the father [Geremio] of his own lie as the earth upon me and mine and must ever by us be borne. . . . Who will not now put food into the open mouths of my little birds? . . . I must live so that they [her family] will *live*. (60)

When Paul and Annunziata return home from the cripple's séance with a "votive light" (158) and a "crucifix" present, both seem to wish a collective family prayer for endurance: "And through their breathless world a consciousness told them that the living do not die" (158).

The sense of a shared communion of difficulties in the Italian family is characteristic of Annunziata, as well as the other women of the community. After Annunziata's conversation with some members of the community about how she will get her family to the Workmen's Compensation Bureau and how she will speak English there, DiDonato writes, "And the women sat in circle, full breast to breast . . . and settled for the evening—the workers' women, the poor with the poor in conversation of life" (144). The endurance of Annunziata and the helping and caring Italian-American community, able to persist under these poor conditions, reminds one much of *Life in the Iron Mills* by Rebecca Harding Davis or of Upton Sinclair's *The Jungle*, where workers live from day to day trying to cope with intolerable conditions and pressures. When Paul is upset about receiving his downgraded, unfair salary of five dollars, Annunziata shows her religious faith in life's trials by saying to him, "It is one Jesu who keeps us living and not their gold, my boy. I would rather starve than for you to weep" (130).

And, finally, the love that Annunziata demonstrates for her husband is unconditional and her desire to continue to raise his children is evident in her prayerlike canticle: "In the home of Geremio, the love of Geremio has become rising mountains" (85). And her prayerlike devotion is beautiful: "But thine [Geremio's] and mine shall not want. My soul shall consume hunger; and my body, [our family's] wall against suffering. On hands and knees shall I glean the earth for their food" (85). When she is dying, Annunziata in her mind desires to dance with Geremio (308). Her love is even more intense if we consider that after Nazone's fall, Paul's nightmare/dream indicates his father's infidelity as is borne out in the corpus of DiDonato's work *(LOA, TCOL, TW)*: "He [Paul] is hurt to think that his father has betrayed Annunziata" (*CC*, 295). In that nightmare, Geremio also appears like a "stranger" who "feigns not to notice him" (295). Paul's father also appears "ashamed" (*CC*, 295).

When I asked DiDonato about *Christ in Concrete*, he said *Christ in Concrete* was his pure work, written while he was young (*DIOM*, 102, 113). In the corpus of DiDonato's literature, if the Geremio in *Christ in Concrete* is the same as the one—the author is sure it is!—who confesses in *The Love of Annunziata* (published in 1941) his infidelity to Annunziata on Holy Thursday, the day before his Good Friday death (*LOA*, 125; see also 135, 136), and who also commits adultery in *This Woman* (*TW*, 35), then it can be seen how great is this Italian woman's forgiveness of her husband. Incidentally, DiDonato's own father (Geremio) had a sexual affair outside of marriage with the wife of the chief of police in the town they lived in.[30] In *Christ in Concrete*, Paul's vision of his father's sin may be considered "pure," since it *only seems* to be present in Paul's dream/nightmare (295). However, in DiDonato's later novels, *Three Circles of Light*, *This Woman* and his play, *The Love of Annunziata*, there seems to be greater confirmation of the existence in reality of his father's sin of adultery, as the chapters on these works show. In other words, the dream/nightmare of Paul in *Christ in Concrete* (295) seems to become reality or come true in these later works of DiDonato's longer fiction and drama. Certainly, Geremio's "sin" of adultery and his fall and death are crucial to the understanding of the corpus of DiDonato's work, his life and the development of his autobiographical character, Paul.

The third message of *Christ in Concrete* helps us to understand the whole corpus of DiDonato's fictional and dramatic work. As has been said, Geremio's fall to death also appears in *The Love of Annunziata*, *Three Circles*, and *This Woman*. Its importance is even obvious in DiDonato's narrative essay, "Christ in Plastic." In addition, Paul's nightmare/dream in *Christ in Concrete* (292–95), mentioned above, is crucial, for it helps us understand the conflicts and resolutions within all these works.

Understood in Freudian terms, the love and hate Paul experiences in his dream/nightmare in *Christ in Concrete* (295) is to become central to the corpus of DiDonato's works. In this dream/nightmare, Paul takes his "ashamed, stranger" father, who has "betrayed Annunziata," back to "Annunziata and the children [home] without hurting his feelings" (295). "He [Paul] loves his father. . . . He walks with him" (295). Paul also admires the physical appearance of his father as he says to him, "You are the only man in the world for her [Annunziata]" (295). The idea in this dream that his father "betrayed Annunziata" (*CC*, 295) and that Paul showed his love in desiring to forgive his father is central to DiDonato's other works, especially his longer fiction and his drama, *The Love of Annunziata*. Geremio's sin of adultery and his fall from the scaffold will play a role in the development not only of Paul's love/hate relationship with his father but also of Paul's relationship with other people. These events in Paul's life will also influence his own relationship with Annunziata, and as indicated, they will play a role in the development of the plots and messages of DiDonato's other works mentioned above.

Another concept mentioned in Paul's dream/nightmare is to prove crucial: "refusing to die" (297). In this dream/nightmare, before Paul falls off the scaffold as his father did in real life and also in this dream,

Paul yells to everyone who is apathetic and who refuses to act as the walls collapse, "Refuse to die" (297). In *This Woman*, as Annunziata forgives Geremio, so does Paul learn to forgive, though through agony. In the corpus of DiDonato's literature, for Paul or any character to develop most fully, he or she must take on a Father and Mother, a male and female component, as the author has constantly propounded.[31] Paul, in the nightmare, falls and wonders if he is his father (*CC*, 297). Certainly Paul empathizes with his father, but he, too, fears he will die similarly in a fall. To overcome this fear and to forgive his father for his wrongdoing takes courage. Therefore, to "refuse to die" (*CC*, 297), in DiDonato's works, invariably means to forgive or to be forgiven, to love or to be loved, or to return "home." In *This Woman*, Paul forgives his father and accepts his mother. Even in *Three Circles*, which portrays both Annunziata and Geremio negatively on the whole, though with positive elements as well, Annunziata still says that her dead husband is building a "home," but it won't be complete until Geremio's children have children and until Geremio's children "ceaselessly pray" (*TCOL*, 244). "Home" is where one is taken to love or to be loved, in the Italian-American experience and in the truest universal psychological experience.[32] "Home" represents self-identity and self-love. To return "home" is to die to one's guilt, to one's past and to one's sins. Geremio's death, expressed as absence from "home," is evident in Paul's words in the dream/nightmare in *Christ in Concrete*: "Where have you [Geremio] been living and what have you been doing? Where have you been this long time?" (295). But then Geremio is "resurrected" [comes alive] in Paul's dream, and he is brought home to Annunziata (295). In Paul's dream, at least, his father seems to be forgiven, loved and accepted. However, as the author will try to develop, it would take the whole corpus of DiDonato's literature for Paul's dream/nightmare to become reality. In *The Love of Annunziata*, where Paul's role is somewhat re-emphasized, Geremio also returns "home" (*LOA*, 136) and is forgiven by Annunziata for his adultery when she dances the Tarantella in her mind as she sits in front of his coffin (*LOA*, 135–36), as has been shown previously. Even in *Three Circles*, in the funeral scene where we probably see Annunziata described as being angry in the most extensive and detailed manner of any of DiDonato's works, when she expresses knowledge of Geremio's adultery with Delia Dunn, Annunziata still forgives Geremio as long as he returns "home to [his] children" (*TCOL*, 135; 201–2; 211, 212, 216). By loving Geremio, Annunziata in *Christ in Concrete* "resurrects" him even though he lies dead before her in a coffin (see also *The Love of Annunziata*). In these words she forgives

Geremio! However, in *Three Circles*, she displays more anger with Geremio's sin. As she does the tarantella in *Three Circles*, she grabs the hat of Delia Dunn, Geremio's lover, and dances the tarantella, but in her attempt to forgive Geremio, she topples Geremio's coffin and beats on it (*TCOL*, 239, 240). Thus, in *Three Circles*, Annunziata's anger at Geremio's sin is most pronounced and evident. Nevertheless, the emotions of love and hate are both still part of Annunziata's reaction even in *Three Circles*.

Likewise, Paul makes a love/hate effort to bring himself home in *Christ in Concrete* at the end of the novel: "He wandered. Not knowing where. Beyond his stun noises went off.... Stupid world. Indifferent.... At Tenement (home) he found himself" (306). Paul returns home to crush Annunziata's "wooden cross" (304–5), and, though angry, she forgives him, nevertheless (305–7). Paul then leaves and returns and is forgiven a second time as he says, "Mama... forgive.... Mama, you made me... I am you in everything" (307). Still later, as stated previously, Annunziata forgives him and makes the prediction that he will have children and be blessed with "the flower of womankind" (309–11). So loving is Annunziata that she even asks Paul for forgiveness (309–11).

Though Paul takes on a Mother, the female component, in *Christ in Concrete*, he is still so young. The nightmare/dream in *Christ in Concrete* (292–98) leaves some question about how Paul will have to resolve the idea of the dream that his father "betrayed Annunziata" (295). It will take the rest of the corpus of DiDonato's literature for Paul to resolve this conflict with his father, what I consider the taking on of the male component. I believe, however, that Paul takes on both a male and female component in *This Woman*, the pinnacle of DiDonato's works. In *This Woman*, Paul finally does come "home." In the chapter on *This Woman*, I show how Paul, like his father in the dream/nightmare of *Christ in Concrete* (292–98), returns "home" when Paul, maturely, through agony and joy, accepts his role as father of his own children and husband of Isa, "the flower of womankind," as predicted in *Christ in Concrete* by Annunziata (311). But in order to do this, Paul has to forgive himself and accept his wife. He has to "forget" or let go of the sin of his father (adultery)—"The wages of sin is death"; "his father's death is the wages of sin"—and cease to commit the sins of his father (*TCOL*, 245; *TW*, 37, 39).

In *This Woman*, for Paul to accept himself as a man, he has to establish his masculinity by not abusing women and by avoiding adultery. As stated in the previous chapter, Paul in *This Woman* has to follow Annunziata's wish at the end of *Christ in Concrete* to seek "the flower of womankind" (311) to be blessed with children (*CC*, 311; *TCOL*, 244). To become a man, Paul has to take on his Mother (the female component) and his sister's purity, love and compassion (also the female component) and to take on his Father (the male component). To do this, he has to take on the positive aspects of a father at "home," rather than to be negatively influenced by an unfaithful, adulterous father. In *Three Circles*, in her most loving moments, Annunziata says Father is building a "true home" (*TCOL*, 244) in heaven. She says this home "will not be complete" until she is old "and until ye [her children] are men and women with children of thy own" and until you "ceaselessly pray" (*TCOL*, 244). In *This Woman*, Paul has to accept the best of Geremio's life and to forgive the worst of Geremio's life (his sin; the consequences of his death). Paul has to do this before he can accept himself. By accepting the most positive aspects of his father, Paul, in *This Woman*, forgives the worst of Geremio's life, and he takes on a Father, the male component. By fulfilling Annunziata's wish made at the end of *Christ in Concrete*, Paul, in *This Woman*, also takes on a Mother, a female component.[33] Once Paul does these things, he is better able to accept his wife and her past marriage and life in *This Woman*. Paul, therefore, dies to his "original sin" and is "resurrected" to life in *This Woman*. The Old Adam becomes the New Adam (Christ) in *This Woman*, but only through much agony, forgiveness, love and compassion.[34]

Paul's "original sin," or sin of doom and guilt, has had to be driven out of his life. We see this sense of doom and guilt in its early development in *Christ in Concrete*, after his father's death, and it reminds one, somewhat, of the stream of American puritanical guilt characteristic of our American literature: "I [Paul] only know I am cheated. . . . Papa's life has been used against me. My toil has been used against me" (303). In the same dream/nightmare, Paul sees his father saying, "Ah, not even the Death can free us, for we are . . . Christ in concrete" (298). In answer to Dorothee von Huene-Greenberg's question in an interview about whether we would be buried alive in concrete, DiDonato answered that even though "fate gets you . . ." (47), "my art is my reprisal" (47)—where "I can see light" (47). DiDonato's corpus of literature manifests the personification of this "light." For Paul to deny death is to develop as a mature man. *This Woman*, to the author, expresses Paul's triumph over death, for Paul's exhortation, made in his dream/nightmare in *Christ in Concrete*, "Refuse to die" (297) becomes *reality* in *This Woman*. Indeed, DiDonato's statement comes true in his art:

Love can shame death (*DIOM*, 105). To not die is to take on a male and female component, a Father and a Mother. For Paul, hate of his father and his father's fate and his own fate was death. In *Three Circles*, Paul is not as open, optimistic, mature or pure as the Paul of *This Woman*. Out of DiDonato's three novels, *Christ in Concrete*, *Three Circles*, and *This Woman*, Paul is most immature and disillusioned in *Three Circles*. In *Three Circles*, Paul does not take on a Father, a male component, for when Paul's mother says, as Bauer points out, that his father is not an "erring father" but "an angel in heaven," Paul cannot accept these statements, for he feels, "The wages of sin is death."[35]

Bauer also points out that Paul loses the innocence of his boyhood in *Three Circles*,[36] and he remains embittered with his father's sin and his own fate. So, in *Three Circles*, Paul does not become whole or take on a male or female component. It is in *This Woman* that Paul first realizes "The wages of sin is death" (*TW*, 39), but he conquers this fear, for he accepts himself, his wife and his family at the end of that novel (*TW*, 220) and he fulfills his mother's promise made in *Christ in Concrete* (311) to be father of a family. Like Isa, Paul's wife, Paul realizes "fear is death" (*TW*, 153). In *Christ in Concrete*, though Paul does ask forgiveness of his mother, the actual forgiving of his father is subtly evident *only* in the dream/nightmare (295) where Paul's love and the beginnings of his hate appear. It would take DiDonato's writing of two more novels, a drama and other works for the Paul of *Christ in Concrete* actually, in the reality (not the dream/nightmare world) of the literary works, to forgive his father and thus take on not only a Mother (the female component), but also a Father (a male component) in *This Woman*. In *The Love of Annunziata*, the three-scene drama, Paul appears more as a "neutral character," with the emphasis being on the development and growth of his mother, Annunziata. Not much information is given in this drama to show Paul as developed as he is in *This Woman*; this, of course, is because Paul is so young in the drama and his role is therefore downplayed. DiDonato seems not to be emphasizing the innocent child in the drama, though Annunziata mentions Geremio's betrayal of her, but this betrayal is downplayed in Annunziata's dance, the tarantella (*LOA*, 134–38; scene 3). Paul does not reconcile this betrayal in *The Love of Annunziata* as he does in *This Woman*.

In conclusion, *Christ in Concrete* is more meaningful than Geduld contends, for it has a "story" with multiple (at least three) "messages" (*DIOM*, 104). First, DiDonato "protests" and "rebels" (*DIOM*, 101) against injustices, especially of those in power, like governments and their agencies and bureaucracies. It is a socioeconomic protest novel of an immigrant people. Second, it is a novel of the "heart,"[37] for it speaks, as Faulkner put it, of the "old verities of truth," or, as we already observed that French put it, of love and compassion,[38] especially in its development of the characters of Nazone, Paul's godfather, and Paul's mother, Annunziata, but also of Paul and other characters. Third, the novel gives us information which helps us in understanding the corpus of DiDonato's work, especially *This Woman*, *Three Circles of Light*, *The Love* of *Annunziata* and "Christ in Plastic." This understanding helps us to more clearly see at least three stages of development: (1) *Christ in Concrete*—Paul's most innocent development where he begins to sow the seeds of his love/hate relationship to his father and life, especially evidenced in the nightmare/dream (295), which was to become a reality for Paul in other novels; (2) *Three Circles of Light*—Paul's most immature stage where he is left to ponder whether his father's sin ("The wages of sin is death") had, in fact, actually sent him to doom; (3) *This Woman*—Paul's trek or journey of growth through intense agony and joy,[39] where he must cast off his sin of adultery, the sin of his own and his father's past, his sense of guilt and doom, and his intense hatred of his wife and her past, and his hatred of himself. Paul brings forth life and growth from "the flower of deathing" in *This Woman* (214): "And he could tell himself . . . that living was the flowering of deathing" (*TW*, 214).

In *This Woman*, Paul discovers who he is by finding "the flower of womankind" (*CC*, 311) and by discovering his role as Father of the "hearth" and "sacred fire" (*TW*, 220) with children and wife on a beach (*TW*, 220)—which Nazone in Paul's dream/nightmare, incidentally, characterized as "a mission" (294), seeking Christ, a work of beauty on the day he died, when he tried to coax Paul to go home rather than work that day in *Christ in Concrete* (280–83). Paul's dream/nightmare in *Christ in Concrete* of "refusing to die" (297) does become a reality in *This Woman*, for Paul becomes a man in *This Woman*. Indeed, Paul's early wish in *Christ in Concrete* to be Father as he returned from work after his father's death is fulfilled in the corpus of DiDonato's literature, notably in *This Woman*: "O Mother, home I come with Father's hands. . . . Mother, lift your heart and rejoice for Father is in Heaven and we shall rise" (*CC*, 104).

9

Three Circles of Light

Three Circles of Light is helpful to the understanding of Pietro DiDonato's works; in order for us to better understand how DiDonato felt that love can shame death (*DIOM*, 105) and how life can occur in a "mystery" (*DIOM*, 104–5) or in "sacredness" (*DIOM*, 113–14), we need to observe the level of development of Paul in *Three Circles* and contrast it to DiDonato's other works, especially *This Woman*, *Christ in Concrete* and *The Love of Annunziata*. Unfortunately, the words of DiDonato above were not to be realized for Paul in *Three Circles*. As has been indicated elsewhere in the present work, it would take the other novels of DiDonato for Paul to realize in his life the concepts of these statements, especially as he does in the novel *This Woman*.

In my chapter on *Christ in Concrete*, I have tried to show how its third message was vital to an understanding of DiDonato's corpus of literature. Part of that message in *Christ in Concrete* was the dream/nightmare of Paul (295), wherein he says that his father, Geremio, betrayed his mother, Annunziata; despite this betrayal in the dream in *Christ in Concrete*, *Three Circles* is valuable, for it helps the reader understand that this betrayal within the dream actually has some basis for existence in the real world of Paul. *Three Circles* supplies much more information on that exact betrayal of Annunziata and her reaction to it, and the novel also shows that Paul, since he is seen from the point of view of being very young, does not yet forgive his father, nor does he forgive or understand his mother's love/hate relationship with his father, especially her love of his father. In short, out of all DiDonato's novels, *Three Circles* shows Paul at his most imperfect stage of development. At times Paul reminds one of Holden Caulfield of J. D. Salinger's *The Catcher in the Rye* in the sense that he is angry at the state of his world, but he does not do anything to improve his lot, for he cannot—he is too young and immature to do so. As the author has tried to point out, it will take the remainder of the corpus of DiDonato's work to trace the development of Paul's growth. Finally, *Three Circles* is the story of an immature youth and his beginning signs of disillusionment that come with that entrance into manhood and the loss of innocence that inevitably follows.

Another way to explain Paul's development in *Three Circles* is to develop the idea that he fails to take on a Mother, a female component, or a Father, a male component, since he does not fully accept his mother or father. It is the author's belief, stated in chapter 7, that Paul most takes on a Father and a Mother in *This Woman*. In *Christ in Concrete*, Paul takes on a Mother but not a Father. In the play, *The Love of Annunziata*, Paul appears to be somewhat "neutral" in the sense that Annunziata's development or characterization is primarily pursued, though her betrayal by Geremio, her husband, is also mentioned. Indeed, the strong love of Paul's mother is quite evident in the play. For us to understand how Paul fails to take on a Father or a Mother, we need to examine especially the latter part of *Three Circles*, as well as the events leading up to it. The ending of the novel most successfully shows Paul's disillusionment. But we need to trace the development that led up to this disillusionment. The most conspicuous event leading to Paul's disenchantment, his inability to take on a male or female component, is the death of Geremio, his father. In addition, Paul's relationship to Stella L'Africana is also strongly affected by the death of his father. Moreover, Grazia LaCafone's and Annunziata's reactions to Geremio's death also influence young Paul.

Paul's perception of his parents in *Three Circles* helps us understand his detailed, though somewhat imperfect, vision of them. His vision involves his inability to resolve his hate of his father and his lack of patience towards his mother's acceptance of her husband's infidelity. That vision is imperfect because Paul is most imperfect and because he is young. Nevertheless, Paul's perceptions and vision of life provide us with the detailed imperfections of that love relationship between his mother and father. Paul, however, does not reconcile himself to these imperfections in *Three Circles* as he does in *This Woman* and even somewhat in *Christ in Concrete*. Therefore, Paul is at his most imperfect as a person in *Three Circles*. In this sense, his vision of life and perceptions in *Three Circles* are the most juvenile or immature within the corpus of DiDonato's novels and his play.

Since Paul's vision of his mother is most imperfect in *Three Circles*, Paul fails to take on that Mother. Annunziata's love and hate of her husband are portrayed quite fully in *Three Circles*. Annunziata learns quite clearly from Filomena and Terestina that her husband has betrayed her (*TCOL*, 189–90; all page references in this chapter are to *TCOL* unless otherwise specified). Though she becomes defensive about these charges and protective of Geremio (190), her reaction, which will be described later, at the funeral of Geremio, expresses both a love and hate relationship with Geremio. When Paul's "godmother," Delia Dunn, gives birth to Geremio's child, who looks like him (191), Annunziata has the tremendous compulsion to forgive the adulterous sin of Delia and Geremio. Annunziata, making a sign of the cross on the baby's brow, says to Delia at the hospital, "Live and love the gift of your life like your beautiful father for a hundred years" (197). On Holy Thursday, before Geremio's Good Friday death in the fall from the construction scaffold, Geremio admits he has been "unfaithful," and he admits his sin of adultery (211). Annunziata, nevertheless, forgives him: "You [Geremio] are mine, regardless!" (211–12).

Though we get these glimpses of Annunziata's love, we also learn of Annunziata's pain as she discovers her husband's untruthfulness. After the hospital scene, Geremio promises to be faithful to Annunziata (199); however, both Paul and his mother track him down one Saturday evening and find that he enters Delia Dunn's house, thereby breaking his promise of fidelity (200–201). It is interesting to note that the word "circle," which appears in the title of the novel, is mentioned three times in connection with this incident at Delia's house; first where Annunziata indicates that Geremio will "do a circle and the end of the circle will be Delia's house" (200). Later, Annunziata says that Geremio "circled" (201) West Hoboken to see Delia (201). These incidents of betrayal are not mentioned as specifically and as extensively in the remainder of DiDonato's corpus of literature. Though Annunziata tries so hard to forgive Geremio (see *TCOL*, chap. 25, especially), her love, as well as her anger, is graphically depicted in chapter 24 at Geremio's funeral. In DiDonato's other works, Geremio appears in Annunziata's mind as a "stranger" in a theater. She says to Geremio, "Ahhhh, Geremio, I am not like thee. I can dissemble no further" (236). Her anger at his past adulterous activities and her hurt are quite evident in the following phrase:

"And of course, my scampering goat, thou might, as usual, have been playing prime Italian sport between the rapid legs of thy dear-dear American women of the short hair and up-ready skirts—were thou faithful to 'Godmother' Delia Dunn, that bloodless, bleached whore? Hmmmm, even I could do as a whore if I wanted." (237)

But then she reverts to what appears to be more loving behavior: "no offense—the thought came of itself—and it's understood thou art the male animal" (237).

But before Annunziata proceeds to dance the tarantella, which she also did in *The Love of Annunziata* and in *Christ in Concrete*, Annunziata again displays more of her anger at Geremio, "I cannot bear any more buffoonery! Hath thou tried to tear my heart? Art thou satisfied now? Dost thou know thy lies and acting will destroy me? Remember, careful, or my children will revenge!" (*TCOL*, 238). Shortly after this, she dances her Tarantella, but it is not exactly the beneficent tarantella in *Christ in Concrete* or in *The Love of Annunziata*. At this moment of the funeral in *Three Circles*, she appears to dance the tarantella "in painful abandon" to cover up her hurt and angry feelings toward Geremio. She lunges at the coffin, "beats her hands upon Father" and "overthrows" the coffin and also lunges at her children (*TCOL*, 240). This picture of Annunziata in *Three Circles* is more detailed and shows someone much less perfect than in DiDonato's other works, and it portrays a mother who both loves and hates her husband. This portrayal also reveals more completely the source of these emotions—Geremio's betrayal.

Paul's view of Annunziata as being less than perfect in *Three Circles* helps us understand his later rejection of his mother. After visiting the medium Sabinella La Zoppa, Annunziata says to Paul, in the form of a prayer, that his father did not die, but is in heaven with the angels, the Virgin Mary and God (244–45). She also says he is building his "final home" (244) there, and it won't be complete until Annunziata's children have children of their own, until she is old, and until the children "ceaselessly pray" (244). Much of the content of Annunziata's prayer and the use of the title of the novel were probably based on Dante's Canto 33 of the Paradiso of *The Divine Comedy*. However, Paul cannot and will not accept his mother's prayer: "We [the Geremio family] had been punished by Heaven for Father's immorality, as 'religion' constantly cried that the wages of sin was death" (*TCOL*, 245). Paul's rejection of his mother comes as a rejection of her religion in *Three Circles*: "The God of my mother and people, who was before but a motionless statue on a cross, beckoned to me and embraced me. All that had been beautiful was now wrong, sinful, grotesque. I was afraid, deeply afraid, of Christ and the world of man" (*TCOL*, 246). It is the author's belief that it is not until *This Woman* that Paul most fully eliminates this fear and accepts his mother, though he does accept her in *Christ in Concrete*, also. Thus, Paul's reaction to Annunziata's prayer is a rejection of Annunziata's religion, her compassion, her forgiveness, especially of Geremio's adulterous sin with Delia Dunn. Paul will have to wait for *This Woman* to forgive another woman, his wife, Isa Tromm, to take on a Mother, a female component. Paul must conquer this fear of the world to take on a female component. He simply lacks the courage at this point in *Three Circles*, and he will not conquer this fear by the end of the novel, either.

In understanding Paul, just as important as Paul's rejection of the female component is Paul's rejection of the male component. In Paul's dream/nightmare in *Christ in Concrete* (295), Paul sees his "ashamed" father, and he forgives him (295). In *Three Circles*, however, Paul does not forgive his father, and therefore does not take on a Father, a male component. After Paul dreams of Sister Alma Serena, Geremio apologizes to his son, though Paul does not acknowledge him: "You [Paul] are the son of Geremio. Perhaps I shall never be the man your father should be.... I am ashamed ... forgive me, my son" (*TCOL*, 216). Paul, however, does not respond by forgiving his father. Chapters 23, 24 and 25 follow, and we are left with Paul's final statement in Chapter 25 of his being punished for his "Father's immorality" (245). Paul's inability to accept (to forgive) his father's sin indicates his inability to accept his father in *Three Circles*. Unlike Paul in *This Woman*, Paul in *Three Circles* does not reconcile himself to his own sin and his father's sin:

> That night, the sense of sin, and the fear of God, was born within me, the definition of sin that made the memory of Father's affair with Godmother Delia ugly, and the remembrance of Stella and Pasqualino in the hayloft, an unclean picture, and my beauteous Stella [his first sexual experience at fourteen] was now an evil, carnal woman, and my pure desire for Stella a dread thing imperiling my mysterious soul. (246)

Not until the ending of *This Woman* does "woman" take on a more respectable role depicted in Annunziata's prediction in *Christ in Concrete* that Paul would participate in the "flowering of mankind" (*CC*, 313)

Paul's guilt also plays an important role in not allowing him to fully develop in *Three Circles*. Paul feels guilty that he told his father and thereby the Italian community of Stella's romance with Pasqualino, her stepson, for it brought about the suicide of her aged husband, Sebastiano, and the death of Pasqualino by Sebastiano. In addition, his father's death has left Paul feeling guilty and afraid of sin (245–46). Paul also wishes he could have stopped his father from going to work on Good Friday, the day he died (221–27). If his father had not died, Paul feels "my [his] life would have been a different story" (221). The dream of being Stella's lover and husband fled with Stella (232) when his father dies (226) and when Grazia LaCafone banishes her from Geremio's funeral (230, 231).

It is only in *This Woman* that Paul restores his courage to accept the future and to forget his own sin, as well as his father's sins. Paul in *Three Circles* is bowed down with guilt and evil: "Reason being removed from love as the earth from the stars, we [Paul and the family of Geremio] sought in vain the image of Father" (221). Not until Paul himself becomes father on the beach in *This Woman* does Paul take on a displaced Father. *Three Circles* shows Paul as Old Adam. *This Woman* shows Paul redeemed through death as New Adam: the fulfillment of Annunziata's angelic prayer in *Three Circles* that her children will bear children (244), and the fulfillment of that same wish in *Christ in Concrete* (311).

Paul's concern with losing Stella L'Africana as a result of his father's death and sin seems to override his loss of Father and his love of Father. Paul here seems overly egocentric:

> But I [Paul] was only a boy about to reach a foot onto the threshold of young manhood. (*TCOL,* 226)

> The darkness, which was to remain for decades about me, lowered to envelop the sunshine of the smiling, early, free, happy, laughing days, and my priceless boyhood fled in terror from me without lingering look or farewell. (*TCOL,* 246)

The "behorned satyr" (246) above Pellegrini's drug store, where Paul had worked as a child, appears in the final paragraph of *Three Circles* (*TCOL,* 246), and it represents the loss of innocence that comes with the knowledge of sin and the consequences of that knowledge, very similar to what Old Adam felt in the Garden of Eden. Paul is, therefore, not redeemed in *Three Circles*. His knowledge of evil is too heavy to be eliminated. Paul's sin before his loss of innocence was his father's sin as once described by Annunziata at her most forgiving moment in the funeral scene where she also displays her anger with Geremio: "My little Geremio forgot to grow up and knows not sin from virtue" (*TCOL,* 238).

Two characters also play a part in the loss of innocence in immature Paul: Annunziata, by her religiosity, as has been explained; and Grazia LaCafone, who can be seen as representing justice and a sense of knowledge of the consequences of sin. Grazia's most marked influence is felt at the funeral of Geremio. She certainly contributes to moving Paul to his "dark" (246) state of loss of innocence. She acts as judge and jury who "sentences" Paul as well as others. It is also interesting to note that she refers to herself as "this woman" when she petitions Geremio's corpse to forgive her for always wanting Geremio (232). Certainly a case could be made that at the end of the novel Grazia represents the voice of strong moral responsibility and, if this is true, then one could understand how DiDonato might have designated the title of his second novel as *This Woman*, since Paul does come to some sense of moral responsibility in *This Woman* after a reckless past. Grazia LaCafone serves at least three purposes in the novel: she banishes Stella from Paul's life; she chastises Paul's actions, and she is instrumental in introducing Paul into a state of loss of innocence. Grazia sees Geremio's affair with Delia as an invalid attempt of an Italian-American to be Americanized. Grazia chastises and then banishes Stella, Paul's first partner in a sexual affair, who comes to Geremio's funeral holding Paul's hand (*TCOL*, 229):

"Have you already taken this child to your corrupting mattress? You, Stella L'Africana, may linger at funeral if you keep tongue between legs. But when Geremio the Dead is earthed, I will see to it that you remove yourself from us paesanos and go at large. Then, come no more near the widow Annunziata's son. Leave unsullied his cross or I will tear you from mouth to fig!" (*TCOL*, 230–31)

Next, Grazia shatters the symbols of Paul's youth, his BB gun, his crystal radio set, and his father's guitar: "Soon bricks, mortar, aches, sweat, trowel and danger will be your toys" (230). Grazia, seeing Paul well dressed, also grabs and snatches his wristwatch and ring, chastising Geremio's affair with the American from Tennessee, Delia Dunn:

"Wouldst Americanize yourself like 'Jerry Philips' [Geremio's stage name since he and Delia danced and played music in the theater, notably the Lincoln Theater (235)]? Who lies in the box of the dead, here, 'Jerry Philips' or the Vastese Geremio di Alba? Buttock to buttock with the pasty, braying American savages would your father be, eh? . . . Are the Americans here to pay for Geremio's funeral?" (231)

Grazia also warns Paul of the dangers of pride and of spiritual death: "Geremio was the peacock, and we forthright Vastese. . . . Know you

[Paul], death in summon, makes all common" (*TCOL,* 232). Grazia then destroys the remnants of Geremio's and Delia's song-and-dance episodes. Grazia also rips the song sheets and orders The Horse [another nicknamed Italian] to burn them (230). The Horse also nails three spikes into the keyboard cover, thereby sealing the piano keyboard. Grazia's disapproval of Geremio's sexual affair and dance and music routine with Delia Dunn represents an attempt to shun Geremio's cultural attempt to Americanize himself, a form of prostitution in Grazia's eyes. Grazia's indictment (231–36), as well as Annunziata's indictment of Delia Dunn (237) and Grazia's treatment of Stella and Paul serve as a warning to Paul that "The wages of sin was death" (245).[1]

Finally, Paul in *Three Circles* emerges in "darkness" (246) simply because he does not accept a Father or Mother component. For Paul, love does not shame death, since he is having a difficult time accepting himself and his lot. His world is a world he never made; it is a world whose consequences belie his father's death. Like an Old Adam, Paul's "original sin" is his loss of innocence, his painful realization that what he once thought was not sin but uninhibited, natural passion, now becomes sin with a penalty. The three circles of light, the triple triangle affairs of Geremio and Delia Dunn, Paul and Stella L'Africana and Stella L'Africana, Pasqualino and Sebastiano, are to take their toll, especially on Paul, who "forgot God, laws and parents and people and cleaved to Stella L'Africana" (182). What once was natural, innocent passion for Paul at an earlier stage of *Three Circles,* like the sinners' passion he first viewed in all three triangle love affairs, was to result in the death of Paul's innocence. In *This Woman,* on the other hand, Paul realizes human limitations in the functioning of the world, and he accepts self, wife Isa, and his children. The "sacredness" (*DIOM,* 104–5) and "mystery" (*DIOM,* 104–5) of life cannot occur in *This Woman* until Paul dies to himself, which, the author believes, finally does occur in *This Woman,* fulfilling his dream/nightmare of forgiving his father in *Christ in Concrete* (*CC,* 295). This positive change of Paul in *This Woman* never occurs in *Three Circles.* In *This Woman,* Paul's dream of forgiving his father is fulfilled. Nevertheless, *Three Circles* is vital in the corpus of DiDonato's literature, for it shows how much Paul needed to grow. Thus, it would take *This Woman* to illustrate that when "reason" is *not* removed from "love" like the "earth" not being removed from the "stars" (*TCOL,* 241), Paul would become whole and come "home" (*TCOL,* 241). In *Three Circles,* Paul is not whole, and he will have to go a long way before finding "home."

10
Conclusion

In studying American literature, especially Hawthorne's works, the author came to understand the sense of puritanical guilt which can forecast doom. At first, a striking similarity occurred for him in reading DiDonato. In presenting his ethnic Italian-American roots, he not only described the sense of guilt that comes with the victimization of such an ethnic group, but he also then presented a sense of psychological victimization which cannot be resolved until the victim loves self and others. DiDonato's corpus of literature has been for the author a triumph of the spirit of love, best manifested in the autobiographical character, Paul, his family and his ethnic community. Paul, a New Adam, represents hope instead of doom.

Acceptance of self and peace within self are somehow dependent on how we view ourselves in time.[1] Examining our efforts to discover ourselves, one is reminded of Charles Olson's statement that a writer must never forget where his roots are—they are in the earth. In tracing this search for one's roots, one's elemental being, DiDonato as writer and person demonstrates that the search often involves pain and agony.[2] As DiDonato's autobiographical character, Paul, searches for self in the three novels and one drama, we note that he, at times, comes close to spiritually dying, but, in the final analysis, he truly lives, as he exemplifies the beliefs of his author that love can shame death (*DIOM*, 105).

Living as Italian-Americans, DiDonato and Paul learned very early the world of socioeconomic oppression. DiDonato's *Christ in Concrete* and "Christ in Plastic" best display this victimization by an abuser and how it can undermine any group or person (*DIOM*, 99–103). But this same victimization, the author believes, was to make Paul stronger because in order for him to survive he had to overcome this ethnic guilt in addition to a psychological guilt which was part of his inherited sin (original sin) of his father. Thus, the Old Adam had to become New Adam. In accepting and overcoming the sins of his past and his father's past, some of them of adultery, Paul learned how to accept himself and his wife (*This Woman*). In this very acceptance, he best represents his mother's compassion (the female component) and his father's strength, industry and courage in facing life (the male component). Thus, these Jungian concepts figure closely in understanding Paul and DiDonato's works.

Another concept shared by Jung and DiDonato was to figure prominently in DiDonato's works—that dreams can make sense (*DIOM*, 102-3) and can help one. In the case of Mother Cabrini and Alessandro Serenelli of *The Penitent*, we see how their dreams made them better persons. In addition, what may very well have saved Paul was the dream/nightmare he first had in *Christ in Concrete* (292–98)—that he would bring his father home and save him from embarrassment of his sin of adultery. I have demonstrated how Paul saved himself by taking on a Father in *This Woman*.

When Paul and Alessandro Serenelli were at their worst stages in life, their perceptions of time were self-destructive (see Lynch). In overcoming this sense of doom, they became New Adams who overcame their sense of guilt within time.

In interviewing DiDonato, I discovered no author is perfect; he is fallible, as is any person. However, in DiDonato's effort to create his art within the milieu of time, he strives to make a better world, for at the foundation of his art is love. Paul, as well as other characters within DiDonato's corpus, is the exemplification of this power of love.

In our effort to discover ourselves or find our roots, what we sometimes discover is hatred of self and other people. But DiDonato's corpus of literature demonstrates that his artistic message is that we can, like New Adams, save ourselves from these darker demons[3]—love can shame death (*DIOM*, 105). DiDonato's works are like his dreams—they offer us the same anguish and hope that Paul's dream of his father offered him: salvation through love, though through agony and pain, the journey of salvation often mentioned by Maud Bodkin and William F. Lynch. In interviewing DiDonato, I discovered some of this anguish and joy. In reading DiDonato's works, I found what was for Suzanne K. Langer the source of artistic imagination: "Self-knowledge, insight into all phases of life and mind, spring from artistic imagination. That is the cognitive value of the arts."[4] In creating his corpus of literature, DiDonato's artistic efforts point out the value of this "self-knowledge" and "insight," especially in the development of the autobiographical character Paul. This "self-knowledge" and "insight" lead to love of self and others, as it did for Paul and for other characters within the corpus.

APPENDIX A
Personal Interview, 14 August 1990

Edited and Partially Translated by M. Diomede

PARTICIPANTS:

P.D.: Pietro DiDonato
M.D.: Matt Diomede
B.D.: Barbara Diomede, the author's wife
F.D.: Frank Diomede, the author's father
J.D.: Josephine Diomede, the author's mother

M.D.: Yes, I just had a number of questions prepared. But I was wondering if you could just talk about your writing a bit.

P.D.: Oh, sure ... just ... Well, you'll get all that material in order in the interview in *MELUS* (von Huene Greenberg) ... I think, in general, that all creative writers have the same problems or concerns: with sex; with the form of government under which they live; with the abracadabra bugaboo of religion; and the dizzying realization of the planets; of hate; of "There but for the grace of Nature go I." When I look at an ant or a repulsive snake or some pathetic animal that is being eaten or swallowed by another animal, and then I ... The creative mind works by contrast and similarities—you know, whatever is similar? It's a sort of computer action. Talking about the animals devouring each other, then immediately comes to mind American boys in My Lai raping and killing people that they don't know! And then what does that lead to? That leads inevitably to what indicates that there are only two classes of men: there are masters and there are slaves. There are predators and there are prey. But there is complicity, though. It's like the story I just got through writing; that there seems to be some kind of fantasy relationship between the oppressor and the victim, because the victim doesn't rebel; he conforms, and you can almost then go into psychoanalysis and associate it with masochism and sadism. And then what does that involve? It involves genesis, a Jew-God that creates the world; it comes out of nowhere, and before the day was over, has invented death and has condemned them to death because they disobeyed his fucking "You shall eat only from the tree of life but not from that tree over there—the tree of knowledge of good and evil." And then upon the scene appears the snake—the serpent. Well, then, when you come to reason it out, you say, "Why did he create the Satan?" There must be collusion between the two of them because one doesn't kill the other one, and yet in between, these pathetic, fragile mortals, they are victimized by both of them!

M.D.: So this victimization is dangerous—extremely dangerous?

P.D.: Oh, sure, sure, sure. And, for example, what's transpiring right now on your television set. These high school and college assholes are going in uniform, invading the Mideast with no ethical, logical, legitimate reason to commit what may be inevitable mass slaughter of civilians, of people who had nothing to do with the oil or are not even profiting by the oil, or any of that. So then, what does that tell you? It tells you that money in action—money is god, that the only valid thing is money, that money is power; and for that people will make war, people will sell drugs, women will prostitute their flesh, and so on. So, in this couple of pages here from "The Creative Person"—it was just by inadvertence that I . . . In these couple of pages here from "The Creative Person" [Donald W. MacKinnon, "What Makes a Person Creative?" *Saturday Review,* 10 February 1962, 15–17; 69], it was just by inadvertence that I went into the filing cabinet that I hadn't looked into in years and found a lost manuscript of a novel. It was under my nose all the while, but I'm so unsystematic, I looked in every place but there. It's called *A Venus Odyssey*—378 pages of . . . What it is all about? It's the response that people have often said to me, "What a colorful speaker you are! You've told so many stories that you haven't written. Like Jack Kennedy said to me in the White House, "Why don't you write that, Pietro?" I said, "Well, do I dare?" He says, "This is democracy." So I wrote it and it was published in *Playboy.* So I put all this material together . . . people were saying, "Why don't you write about what happened to you?" I thought, "Oh, I'm not going to make up any stuff"—so your sexual experiences, your sexual vagaries . . . so I called it *The Venus Odyssey.* Because to me the only God that I have now is beauty and my wife who died as my God. Even though my *Immigrant Saint*, a beautiful book about life, about Mother Cabrini, is coming out again, this time by St. Martin's Press; but I'm justified in bringing that out at the same time expressing myself the way I am, because when I write about religion, I do not write about this Jew on the cross or the Jew in the skies. I write about my father, my mother, and Mother Cabrini whom I know indirectly because I've interviewed all nuns who were her postulants. We know she was here. We can see the hospitals she built, and the orphanages, and the parishes that she was responsible for—the good that she did, like Mother Theresa [in India]. And it does not matter whether Mother Theresa or Mother Cabrini believed in Jesus Christ, or Bob Haoula, or what;

it's the good that they did for their fellow human beings; that's all that matters. For example, one night I presented Angelo Roncalli, Pope John XXIII, the beautiful hand-tooled light leather and gold special-made copy by McGraw Hill of the *Immigrant Saint*. I autographed it to him; and then we talked and talked for a while. I said in my Abruzzaze dialect in Italian, "*Ma tu credi che quando muori ti trovi abbracciazo quel fallegname Ebreo?*" ["But do you believe that when you die, you will embrace that Hebrew carpenter Christ?"], and he said to me, "*Ah, Figliomio, speriamo*" ["Oh, my son, let us hope"]. At least he didn't say, "*Oh, certamente, Gesu m'aspetta io Papa*" ["Oh, certainly, Jesus is waiting for me; I am the Pope"]. You're humans. Like my darling, shortly before she died, I didn't tell her that she had cancer. So she had some strokes, most cerebral, and she had severe dementia but she never lost her perceptions about my identity, and I didn't tell her that she had massive cancer. I wanted to prepare her. I'm a blabbermouth. My sons said, "Don't you dare tell mother." So I said, "Dear . . ." and she said, "Oh, we must get in touch with Mother" [her mother]. I said, "Your mother has been dead twenty-five years. . . . But you know, dear, it won't be long you, she and I will meet [said emotionally] somewhere"; and she said, "Who knows, who knows?" Then a little later she died in my arms. But there was still that honesty, see what I mean, her character. If you don't know, then you cannot lie to yourself. I think that has all the divinity of truth. You cannot change human nature; you cannot educate the masses. Voltaire said it before me: he said, "As long as man believes in myths and absurdities, he will continue to commit atrocities"—and that is true. In the name of this Jew Christ, how many people have been tortured, flayed, decapitated, and what not? And the Puritans who came here and what they did to the Indians, and what the Huguenots did to the Calvinists, and what the Calvinists did to each other—Cromwell and the rest. Cromwell went and killed little babies and children. He said he did it because nits would become lice. So you see, you inevitably must gather that I am a protester; that I am a missionary of my own sense of rebellion and violation of the injustice to us, poor, fragile creatures who will live here so briefly. Whereas, if we loved each other, it would be a fucking paradise! It would be a paradise! But every generation or even sooner than . . . every decade it's like the woman's monthly menstrual flow. They have to go and commit bloodshed. Leave their fucking homes, the children, go ten thousand miles away and play soldier boys! They're all culpable, all races. The Communists turned out to be fiends. The Nazis made no bones about being fiends. The Americans are the biggest hypocrites of all—these puritanical, self-righteous exploiters—and you'd think that they would stop doing it. No. They just find new ways of . . . now that . . . for instance we're right back to double-speak. We're right back to Orwell. That wasn't his real name. I forgot his real name, but anyway we'll call him Orwell—the '84 stuff—the blockade. They're going to blockade the Iraqis. What that means is their children won't get food, medicine, and this and that. What's the children got to do with what they're doing? But it's not a blockade; it's an interdiction. That's like the story of the black woman who went to the black doctor. And she was good-looking, and he was a big buck, and he looked at her and he said, "I'll have to examine your vagina"; and then he said, "That's a serious, serious condition y'all got." He then said, "I'm gonna have to do something very, very special. It's not going to cost you . . . well, it's going to cost you a lot of money, but I'll do it, only special for you." She said, "What's that?" He said, "It's a process called fornication." She said, "Must you do it?" He says, "Yeah." And while he is doing it, she said, "Doctor, if you hadn't told me you was fornicating me, I'd swear you was fucking me." So he says, "This asshole nigger-son of the rich people will protect us." He says, "Is that a blockade? Interdiction." I tell you, the grotesquerie of it all provokes my laughter, because all ugly things are funny. Comedy is funny and all beauty makes me weep for joy—a beautiful woman, a beautiful child, a beautiful day, my cat who loves me. So you say, "How does a person write?" You write because all these scenes overcrowd the cerebral warehouse, whatever you want to call it, the mind. There has to be a catharsis; it has to be. Why did I write *Christ in Concrete*? Because I dream every night and I'm on jobs that's . . . last night I dreamed—I can't get away from it. I have no control over my . . . Do you have any control over your sleeping world? No one has. I'm always laying bricks, I'm always falling off scaffolds, I'm always saving my father. . . . My father's death weighed on me and so forth and so on. *Christ in Concrete* was the easiest thing that I ever wrote and the best thing I ever wrote. It had many things in its favor. The boy was pure, he was a virgin, he was a little saint, I was. But we don't remain that way; we grow up and so forth. Then these things bother you and in order to cope with it, you write it. You get it out of your system. Why else would a man write? Of course, once he becomes known and becomes a success, that's a different story. Then he has the success hanging over his head whether he doesn't write another best-seller, short of a fall, and destroy him, so forth and so on and that of course . . . Who the hell is going to sympathize with that? Who's going to sympathize with a man who has risen above the crowds?

M.D.: That's one question I had, and it was maybe dealing with *The Penitent*, like, how do you use the dream in your works? You kind of filled in just now that . . .

P.D.: Yeah, yeah, yeah. We cannot disregard the dream world. It's a sort of a kaleidoscope. You know how the unpredictable ways in which mistakes will fall into patterns? And the dream world is like that, because many times it doesn't make sense, but many times it makes terrible sense. Dreams where they're about to rape your wife before your eyes and then you see a cop and you run to the cop, you find out the cop is with one of them and things like that. There's also the fear of death. We're all doomed. We're all tragedies. My friend down the corner here. He just died. He was a test pilot for Grumman, paralyzed for a couple of years. But his wife believes that he has gone to heaven. She says, "What's the use of living, then; this is not the answer?" she says, and so forth and so on. I said, "They're all tragedies." The moment that your child comes into the world reminds me of when I was in Conscientious Objectors Camp up in Cooperstown, the Second World War, that's where I met my widow. My wife was a young widow. There was an Italian saloon keeper. For years he had worked on the railroads, and he had retired and opened up a saloon. He was a giant of a man with a mustache. It happened in that day that his son, Carminuccio, was leaving for the front. His gypsy of a white-haired wife, she was standing looking out the plate glass window with a ceiling. She wouldn't look at her son or husband; she was just turned to stone. And he was drinking out of his daily fifth of Three Feathers and an anisette. He drank a fifth of anisette. The kid said, "*Papa, mi vai non sacc'o quanno ritornare* [I go (to war): I do not know when I will return]. His father grabbed one of his hands, opened up the cash register, took a roll of cash and stuck it in the fists of his son. And with the other hand he pulled him towards him with tears in his eyes. "*Ti hai pigliato e lacreme*" [You have taken my tears]. Where the hell did fucking America conjure language like that? "*Te si piglata e lacreme?*" [Did you take my tears?] because you know that love holds you hostage. You know damn well that somewhere along the line that baby that was shot or that baby that was in that automobile accident might have been your baby—might have been your grandson, grandchild.

M.D.: Sounds like when my dad came to visit me one month about 1980, 1982, and my father was leaving on the airport ramp, and my mother was already down there; he wouldn't leave. And I'm pushing him on the ramp to go back to New York, and he starts crying. Yeah, he came to visit us about two years ago.

P.D.: That's wonderful that you have your parents. That's . . . I lost my father when I was twelve. My wife lost hers . . . he was only thirty-six; and Helen lost her father, an officer in the Air Force in the First World War. His plane crashed two days before Armistice Day. He died on Armistice Day. She was nine years old. And then my mother died nine years later. She was the same age as my father when she died. She was forty-four. That was nine years later, of her cancer. Then my sister, who was the mother to all of those kids, seven brothers and sisters and I. I was the father; I was the supporter of my family. I supported everybody and she . . . I became famous overnight [from *Christ in Concrete*]. The Book of the Month Club took my book *Christ in Concrete* over *The Grapes of Wrath*, and I was famous overnight and I had money. A couple of months later, she dies of an embolism in a New York hospital, after a gall bladder operation. She was older. Then, . . . I was twenty-nine or so. She was two years older. So you know, who are you going to turn to? Who are you going to say: You dirty bastard God, when there is no God? There's no God. There's nothing. We're being ridiculous. A Jew? Or on the form of what? I thought God was—Jesus—was an Italian. I thought his father was an Italian. I thought his mother, La Madonna, was . . . because we have all those pictures in our tenement flat there, you know. Jesu, this and that. I found out that he was also a Christ killer. So I tell you, the more you learn, the more insane you become. The more you read the Bible, oh, Christ's sake! It's scandalous! The presumption, the lies. . . . When you find out that long before the Jesus Era, that long before the Old-Testament-of-Genesis deluge, there were deluges in the other religions thousands of years earlier and there were fires and volcanoes.

M.D.: Is Paul, Paolo, in *Christ in Concrete* autobiographical?

P.D.: Oh, sure.

M.D.: O.K. At the end . . . you smash the crucifix, right? Is there a turnaround in Paul, a new relationship in Paul, a new relationship with the mother at the end? The end of that is beautiful.

P.D.: Well, she didn't die then, but I forgot. Did she die then? No, I don't think so.

M.D.: No.

P.D.: But I understand what it meant to her. I didn't persevere, I didn't say that, and I didn't say anything like that; in fact, I went ahead and had my confirmation after that. Because I knew to take that away from her would have been cruel.

M.D.: Yeah, there's a strong love of the mother.

P.D.: Well, I mean because Jesus was part of the family. She didn't look on him as a Jew. The religion of those old people as illiterates is beautiful.

M.D.: Could you talk about your process of writing? How you go about writing?

P.D.: Yes, Yes. First of all, I . . . it has to be a story. It has to be also a message. It has to signify something that deals with always, mostly, inevitable involuntary compulsions like sex. Sex has been my torment most of my life. And now it's torment because I can't do it. And before, it was torment because I was oversexed. And that still lingered in the sense of sin, even though I was no longer believing in a personal God.

M.D.: You can see that in *Three Circles of Light*, too. More so, I think, than in *Christ in Concrete*.

P.D.: Well, in *Christ in Concrete*, he [Paul] had the indestructibility of innocence. But, of course, we see that the Catholic religion—it tells you when you're seven years old and you get your first Holy Communion, that you're indoctrinated to be a responsible Christian and to know the difference between right and wrong. It's why you're initiated into confession and repentance, contrition and so forth, which I think are good things, good. I mean, we don't have to believe in the Jew god or anything like that. Confession is nothing but telling the truth, that you did something wrong, whether it was against your father, your family, your whatever, or even against yourself, like masturbation and so forth and so on. As I see it, there's no such thing as wise men. We cannot penetrate the mystery of the planets. I mean, here we are whirling in through space right now. We don't know. The equilibrium is so, that whatever it is, you see. You know, you build a house. You got to build it on rock, because rock, you have to blast the rock. If it's dangerous and unsupported you have to drive piles or otherwise spread footing. But then you can put the house on top of that. But here's the earth; what does it rest on? See, oh, God keeps the end of *Divine Comedy* by the love that impels the stars and the planets, you know. I get a kick out of Dante. He never mentions his wife and all his kids. He married a Donati, as you know. The most interesting of all is the "Inferno," where these people get their comeuppance. Now I did that in "The Gospels," which is the title, now she [his agent] changed the title to "The Last Judgment," which she's finding great difficulty in getting a publisher for. Because how can you destroy Christianity in all the religions and destroy the world and then have the last judgment in which they're really, really punished? Those who deserve rewards are immortalized, deified, and become gods, and Venus is our chief divinity. Because, after all, this isn't our mother, our wife, our womb, our vagina or chief divinity? How would I feel it now without my Helen [his wife]? Even though I wrote that book, *This Woman,* about her, now all that, because of my paranoia about . . . it was my Catholic compulsion to have had a virgin wife.

M.D.: What you were trying to do then in your work was . . . it's hard to summarize everything. If we had to succinctly say it, what you were trying to do, what would it be?

P.D.: Well, I tell that in "The Gospels." No matter what we do in life, all takes place within mystery. We cannot . . . to get away from the mystery of life it is like going into outer space where would we . . . we would be catapulted into infinity and never return to our homes.

M.D.: So life has a certain sacredness in that mystery?

P.D.: Yes, yes, yes, yes. I hate to sound corny, but the jewel, the pearl from all of that is love; whether it's the love of your father, or the love of your mother, or the love of your fellow man. With that, you can shame death; you're not afraid to die again and then you say I have loved, I have been loved. That has nothing to do with money or power or sex. He [my wife's husband] loved her, and she didn't want the book published, because I had written about her and her husband marrying her and everything else. It *[This Woman]* is a great book.

M.D.: Your wife?

P.D.: I wrote about my wife.

M.D.: And her husband?

P.D.: Yeah. Her husband was dead. She was a widow before I married her . . .

M.D.: It's a theoretical kind of thing like in the dream.

P.D.: Yeah, yeah. We had lived together and I didn't think I was going to marry her, and I asked her all kinds of questions, her personal life, and everything else. I found out and then . . .

M.D.: Then you put it together imaginatively? . . .

P.D.: It boomeranged on me after I married her. I kept seeing her with the other guy. It's a great book. So I made three, or four, or five copies like this [an unbound copy of *This Woman* that he will give to me since I did not have a copy] and they're bound. So this is unbound because if I want more copies, I'll bring it to the printer and he puts it in and zing, zing, zing, zing. So I thought I had another. You can have this little memento from Mario [Mario Cuomo, then governor of New York].

M.D.: Could you talk about what questions about your work you'd like to have answered? What questions that have not been explored about your work? What questions would you like to see answered about your work or done about your work that maybe might not have been done?

P.D.: I am seriously concerned about the . . . my last work, "The Gospels," which now my agent has retitled "The Last Judgment," in which each Gospel has a different Christ, and it all takes place today. And it's contemporary and I raise all the questions and contradictions that are in these "Gospels." For example, when Christ . . . I know Christ . . . he's . . . every one of my Christs is a Professor of Stony Brook University. The two . . . one is an American Indian and another one is the Jew who returns in the Second Coming, the *Finalmente*. The third one is a Chinese beauty whom I lay on the altar of Saint Peter's because I had always wanted to screw god and she destroys the world as should be destroyed. Then the last, she's Chinese, and she's yellow. We have a red man, we have a white Christ, a red Christ, we have a yellow Christ, the Chinese female, and then the Christ of "Last Judgment" is black. And the "Last Judgment" takes place at the local cinema. All the crimes committed throughout the history of man are reviewed and the trials take place there. The Kent State, the kids are there handing out leaflets for their trial, from their slaughter. Sacco Vanzetti is there. Moses is brought up for genocide, Joshua is there, David is brought up for genocide, Jehovah is brought up for malpractice. But Jehovah defends himself; his plea is that he doesn't exist. The only god that exists is mammon, capitalism. But he's a good god, because capitalism is not in the form of a human being but in a collage of universities and laboratories and workshops and science and inventions—sort of a Prometheus. So it is a fantastic, wonderful, wonderful mythical world and then the fifth Gospel is Paradise. It is the Paradise of Tannhäuser [a musician or minstrel], Venusberg [DiDonato's paradisal kingdom] and all the good human beings throughout the ages who hurt no one, who gave love, are immortalized and are all made gods. And they can renew their virginity every day by bathing in the stream of Kanathos. This is a Greek history, Greek legend. In fact, the village where my DiDonatos come from and Taranta Pellinio, the wood-mill town, where it is alleged that I am the grandson, the bastard grandson, of Gabriel D'Annunzio because he was there and impregnated . . . he fucked my father's mother when she was a young girl; knocked her up and when he was writing his great play, *La Figlia di Iorio* [The daughter of Iorio] . . . I have it upstairs in Italian . . . *La Figlia di Iorio*. I spent some time up in the mountains there in that village. The adjoining mountaintop is the valley, the birthplace and home of Benedetto Croce. Everywhere you turn there is history. It's fabulous! And on that same mountaintop of Croce, if I recall correctly, is still the pagan shrine of Juventas—the goddess who furnishes virility for gods and men. So you see, predating this nonsense of Christianity, there was a natural god, there was nature. And everything was out of the woman's broadest vagina—out of her womb. And that's how my "Gospels" end. That is the Paradise.

M.D.: That's not in print yet, right?

P.D.: Not in print. She loves it. The agent loves it. She represents Kazantzakis, all his work. She's an old woman. She's ninety-eight years old, sharp as can be. It will eventually be published and that is . . . you know when I got the idea? When I read *Villon's Life*. Francis Villon and his beautiful, beautiful poetry which is so real and what a contrast to the fakery of Shakespeare. So you know, Shakespeare imitated Spenser and Marlowe . . . But Villon was . . . in fact, Villon was a century before Shakespeare. He sounds like somebody today, a modern. Well, he wrote his minor testament and his major testament. This was . . . I'd say it was his will. I had determined that "The Gospels" would be my testament. And I finished it. I'll tell you what I'll do, I'll loan you a copy of it; that is important. I've got two copies upstairs bound.

M.D.: I'll xerox that and return that along with the other. OK?

P.D.: Which one?

M.D.: With *This Woman*.

P.D.: Then you are in a position that no one else has all this stuff; you're making this your . . .

M.D.: Yeah, I don't know whether I'm going to concentrate on *Christ in Concrete* or the other, you know. You've answered . . . I had more questions . . .

P.D.: You'll get a hell of a lot of material out of "The Gospels"—how I think, where I am, and all of that.

M.D.: Was your family religious, you kind of answered that. And then I had another question: does the color gray mean anything special in *Christ in Concrete*—gray?

P.D.: Well, it is actually the color of concrete cement. Can you do without cement and construction? [Pietro leaves momentarily to get the manuscripts and returns.] There's nothing like it. It will be published. This is it, "The Gospels" are in here, and this is *This Woman* here.

M.D.: Were the docks in *Christ in Concrete* on the Jersey side, weren't they?

P.D.: Oh, yeah, oh, yeah. So write your name and address and phone number and where you're at and all that sort of stuff. [He looks at my name.] Diomede? Diomede the Greek founded Vasto, Vasto, Piazzo Diomede. Diomede the Greek founded Vasto; my village [Vasto] is older than Rome! Founded it before Rome, like Naples was founded.

M.D.: He founded it?

P.D.: Diomede, the Greek. Not the mythical Greek, the real Greek Diomede founded Vasto. Vasto is not its original name. There was a Latin name; I forgot.

M.D.: This is my work address; all right?

P.D.: Cahokia? [Illinois]

M.D.: Yeah, across the way from St. Louis. And this is my home address. I live on the Missouri side. 815 . . .

P.D.: Is that anywhere near Skokie?

M.D.: Illinois?

P.D.: Yeah.

M.D.: I think Skokie is more near Chicago.

P.D.: You know Skokie? They built a multimillion-dollar Saint Maria Goretti school and church and so forth, and I never went there. They invited me; I never went there.

M.D.: Yeah, I think it might be up near Chicago. My Mom and Dad, eighty years old, took Amtrak to Chicago and then came down to see us with a niece and nephew two years ago; Amtrak all the way. They had never seen any part of the country at all.

P.D.: Well, did they drive this time from . . . ?

M.D.: No, I drove. They're in Hawthorne [New York].

P.D.: You drove your car here, I see. What ferry are you taking back?

M.D.: Port Jeff. [between Long Island and Connecticut].

P.D.: At what time?

M.D.: I think we missed the 4:00 P.M. We were going to head for the 4:00 P.M.; there is a 6:00 P.M. They took a little walk. [My family had returned and were waiting for us to finish the interview.]

P.D.: I see. Well, you can relax and . . .

M.D.: Did you want me to hit you with a couple of more questions, you think?

P.D.: Well, while you're here.

M.D.: Let me get a couple of more in, OK?

P.D.: Yeah, sure, while you're here.

M.D.: Is there a bibliography of your works that you are aware of?

P.D.: Yes, there is, but I don't know really where they are. I've been in so many different American encyclopedias, this, that, and I never kept track; never paid any attention.

M.D.: Ethnic literature is very popular today. What do you see as the advantage or disadvantages, if any, of ethnic literature?

P.D.: Define specifically what you mean by ethnic. You mean Germans and Jews living here? Or you don't mean literature from outside of the United States?

M.D.: No. Concerning the Italian-American immigrant. You may even connect it with this. If there were an Italian experience in America, how would you best characterize or describe what you'd consider the Italian experience in America? —although it is hard to formulate a generalization.

P.D.: You could derive that from my work *Christ in Concrete*. Or w could go on and on. Or the trials and death and murder of Sacco-Vanzetti. Then there's Angelo Pellegrini. You've heard of Angelo Pellegrini?

M.D.: I believe so.

P.D.: Yeah, he'd written books for Knopf on.... In fact, I think I have his address. I got a letter from his wife. We were together at the Italian, the American Italian Historical Association Convention last November [1989]. In California, the Fisherman's Wharf in ... the hotel....

M.D.: Ramada Inn?

P.D.: Ramada Inn, yeah. Ramada Inn. And he's in his eighties, but he's written wonderful stuff. I read some of his books at my brother's house, and I spent the winter with my brother in California. My wife died October 19 and a couple of weeks later I left here. I was so shattered. I went to stay with my brother. And I couldn't ... I have a son in San Jose, a gynecologist, a beautiful fellow ... so Pellegrini is published by Knopf. His father was a railroad worker. I read his stuff. It showed how hard they [the Italians] worked; they were the Asiatics of their day. Like the Asiatics here today—my God, you can't outwork them ... they're the producers. But the ethnic, it depends on the quality of the literature. How much social content it has. Well, the word is "truth," because, regardless of the nationality, if they simply told the truth about their habits, their dreams, their tragedies and their labor. What else, what else? Then you could derive clues and realizations of what constitutes this so-called Americanism.

M.D.: What would you say were the greatest virtues you've acquired from the Italian heritage? In *Christ in Concrete* [I quote], "The endurance of the Italian immigrant" is spoken highly of. Where in your family or neighborhood did you learn this admirable trait of endurance?

P.D.: Right, in my home. No English was spoken, just Italian, and their values were age-old. My mother would not buy anything that was in a can, or all that artificial stuff; it was all fresh. She smelled the chickens' armpits and behinds and everything else and made chicken. The only butcher in Italian was the pork Store, pork and veal, *interiore* [fresh meat from the butcher]. It was wonderful food. We despised the Americans' awful food. We concentrated on vegetables, a lot of garlic, onions ... I still to this day am like that.

M.D.: What part of Italy did your family come from?

P.D.: Abruzzi.

M.D.: Abruzzi, yes. North of Bari. At one point you talk about the tenement, the Jewish ... two boys from Russia. Is that based on fact?

P.D.: This is from *Christ in Concrete*. Oh, yeah, yeah. Well, his [Louis's] brother was a young Communist and he was murdered by the Red Guards. This is how I learned about the communism from Louie. Louis, through me, ended up being in the Agriculture Department. He wanted to study law like his brother who married a rich girl, and she changed from a Communist to a capitalist. I said, "No, if you ... you went to your law school," I said, "you can continue law and then we will no longer be friends. You have to do something that contributes to humanity. I contributed my hands, my child, I build. I want you to bring something out of the earth." So he went to Rutgers to study agriculture. It was during the Depression; he went right from Rutgers into the Agriculture Department and became a noted agricultural economist and ended up after he retired going around the world for the UN.

M.D.: That might tie in with another question I had which was, why do you use the imagery of the earth to characterize the Jewish family in the tenement house? The imagery of the earth?

P.D.: A lot of things come out of the earth. What would we do without earth?

M.D.: What are the main themes in *Christ in Concrete*? Social, justice, economical, political?

P.D.: The struggle of so-called economic survival. The great god Job.

M.D.: Yeah, my father. My father trying to make it.

P.D.: Sure. That's all they talked about. They didn't talk about the country. They talked about the specifics of their work, whether it's the shovel, the pick, or the trowel, or the hammer, the chisel. Who was the foreman and who was the contractor? And the weather. What conditions could you work? It was brutal survival. And the women made preserves during the summer. *Conserva*, stuff in jars and, of course, in the winter there was no welfare, there was no home relief or anything like that. There was the overseer of the poor. That was a joke.

M.D.: On several pages of *Concrete*, you nicely characterized the sense of guilt in the Geremio family. This guilt was characterized as a feeling that they had done something wrong as they return from being treated badly by the Compensation Board. Did the sense of guilt portrayed by Hawthorne or any other American writers influence you, or was the sense of guilt you so ably portrayed part of the Italian immigrant experience, as it is for Arthur Miller in the Jewish experience?

P.D.: You lived it. When you've lived it, you couldn't attribute the maltreatment to anything but maybe something that you represented to them that was maleficent; you were never them. You were a dago, a wop, a greaseball, a guinea.

M.D.: Where and why did you get your interest in writing?

P.D.: There was one instance. There was always a trigger that sets off an atom bomb or lightning that strikes certain places. I had wanted to be an actor. I had run away from home four times before I was ten years old. My mother put me in the drugstore to work after school when I was seven years old. Iorio's drugstore in West Hoboken. I wrote quite a few stories about that.

M.D.: That's in *Christ in Concrete*, the drugstore, I think. *Christ in Concrete*, isn't it?

P.D.: No, I think it's in *Three Circles of Light*; yeah, yeah, yeah.

M.D.: I'm getting them mixed up.

P.D.: That's real, and I made a good living with the trowel and with my knowledge of the blueprints, because I studied at night two or three nights a week at City College in construction and engineering. Even without the benefit of high school, because I had no high school, but in those days, during the boom, it was the burgeoning America. It was Walt Whitman's *Democratic Vistas*. Have you read his *Democratic Vistas*? That's even better than his poetry. You could ... it's sort of like the California atmosphere in a way today. California can bite off more than you can chew regardless of what your color is, your race, your size or what. It was the boom, it was a boom. If you could do it, if you were a monkey, if you could sling a trowel, they would have hired a monkey. Then the Depression came and finally I was about to work in the Depression because I was a master mechanic. I didn't drink, I didn't smoke, I didn't fool around, and then there was no work at all. I was living in this bucolic village on Long Island, Northport. In fact, I brought Thornton Wilder there after I became a celebrity there ... This is our town here, see. I had a friend named Joe Dantz, the carpenter, socialist. I had dragged him to the woman who owned the *Northport Journal*. On top, it said, "The Home of 1500 of the Best People on Earth." She had three daughters. I had my eye on them and I bragged about I was going to open up a summer theater for them. I just shot my mouth off. The following week it was headlines. "Local Resident Opens Up Summer Theater" and it was the old story, "Call a man a dog, and he'll bark." I was so embarrassed! You know, I was penniless and on home relief. But I managed to open up a summer theater. I went through with it. That would make a book or play, or movie ... Oh, Jesus! So I got around with my friends, Jewish friends, and his [Dantz's] father had some money. I got the money from him. So, anyway ...

M.D.: It [*The Love of Annunziata*] was a best one-act play in 1941.

P.D.: No, yes, but that came much later until [sic] I was famous. I wrote that on the Island Pines after many drunken bouts with Hemingway and all that sort of stuff from Havana. But he was talented. So my friend, Joe Dantz, one day said to me, "Pietro, you want to meet a writer?" He said, "My friend, Ben Simco, writes in Greenlawn; he writes plays." I said, "Sure." So he brings me over. I won't go into all the detail; I'll just get right to the point. A writer of a play called *Way Station*. I found out later he was imitating all the stuff that was out before, you know. This play-writer [sic] was imitating. And he said, "I got something for you to read. You don't seem to know anything. You look like a smart guy." He gives me a book called *Awake and Sing* by Clifford Odets. So I took it home and it didn't take me long to read it, and I was disgusted with it—typical Hebrew lamentations in the Bronx; people who ... are in one of the trades, fur trades, etc. It was such a contrast to the virile men like my father and your father: Paesanos, the outdoor, the struggle with big hard jobs—steel and concrete. I said, "My father bought a house the night before he was killed. I picked up the house. He was killed on

Good Friday." And I went back to this guy's house, Ben Simco, and I told him. I said, "I didn't care for that; these people are not noble people; they're whiners in this matter. My father he just wanted a roof over his head for his children, his family. He was denied that." And I said, "He was noble. He was 'Christ in Concrete.'" Of course, I told him my father was caught and collapsed in concrete! He said, "Hey, that's a great title—I think I'll write a story about it." When he said that, that triggered me. I said, "Oh, no." He said, "What?" I said, "I've written it already." I always shoot my mouth off. He said, "I'd like to see it." You'll see, now I am going to write it. I did write it as a catharsis. It didn't take me long, maybe a month. And the funny thing is, I had gotten him a job at WPA because I was teaching drama; here I didn't know my head from a hole in the ground, but drama—I was teaching it because I had a summer theater behind me. And then in the summer I was teaching swimming. I was a great swimmer. The day—we used to meet once a week with the phony director of the activities, and we'd meet and give pep talks and all that so forth. And he said, "I am pleased to announce that one of our teachers here has sold a story to *Esquire* magazine." He looked around; Bing! "Pietro DiDonato sold 'Christ in Concrete.'" We all went through the roof. We were nobody, an ignorant guinea bricklayer—boom! That was 1937 and I was deluged by all kinds of publishers. "Where's your books?" They didn't believe I was a bricklayer and so forth. So then I got a copy . . . Simon Schuster called me. and I didn't have a phone. They wrote a letter and found out my address in Northport. I came in and I had written two chapters. I wrote the funeral, which is the best part of the book, a heartbreak. Prince Howard, the editor, said, "Sorry, Mr. DiDonato, the owners of the company Schuster, Simon Schuster . . ." He said, "This could never make a book" and I said, "Fuck them. This is going to be a book." This determined me, because I saw stupidity. Because I read a lot of shit in other books, when I got his, I thought, "I can do better than that." A friend of mine, Mike Langford, he was rich and he was a screenwriter, and he was summering in Northport with a friend of mine, Israel Feinstein, who later changed his name to I. F. Stone. You know I. F. Stone? He was a great friend of mine, great friend of mine. Mike thought of bringing four chapters to Bobbs-Merrill. Bobbs snapped it up and called me in and gave me a contract—a lot of details. And in eight months I had . . . the President, Mr. Chambers, from Indianapolis, and he came to New York and took me out to lunch and he said, "Pietro, we're not going to tell you how to write that book. We feel that no one can write [your book], but you can write [it]. You have to edit it yourself, because the way you write, it's a different thing." I said, "Well, how do I . . . where do I end?" He said, "When you can't go any further, just put 'The End.'" I did that, every month I took it. Bing! Bing! It's funny, there's always a point in your lives . . . it's almost as if the unforeseen accident occurs. It reminds me of a psychiatrist that ended up with a big name, Jacob Moraino. I met him through Toni's Bistro. The famous Toni Selmar, whose daughter married John Houston . . . and a long, long story. I met Francho, Toni's mother. She was a multimillionaire. She owned Carborundum, Inc., something or other. She bought a Vanderbilt estate up on the Hudson opposite of Beacon. What's opposite of Beacon? Or Jersey there. Anyway, a place you'd know at the opposite . . . shore anyway . . . They invited me up to the "White House." It was called the White House. When I got up there it was a mansion, big wood frame house; it had servants and all that. I said to him, "Why do you call it the White House?" Moraino said, "It's painted white." So I found out later; he was telling everybody I was one of his patients. He would invite you up there, you know, have free drinks, but it was on her tab. She was paying for all this. But Moraino had two things going. He had the psychodrama, the improvised theater. It was nothing but the old Italian *Commedia improvisata*. You played the opposite of what you were. If you were a committed soldier, you played Hitler, and so forth and so on. I could do a book on that. Then he had the other thing called sociometrics. He had a chart there, and they were all lined; it was all lined geometrical. When I meet you, there's a crossing of the lines, something happens. It's like a sperm: sperm life when something takes place somewhere, that certain time. The meeting could be a tragic accident; it could be fortuitous. It could be the right number you win from the guy who sold it to you. I often thought that it was never developed that I know of. But he would cross all these lines. Here's where Diomede crosses Mr. DiDonato. And that's the way it is in life.

M.D.: That's part of that mystery you were talking about. What do you see is the difference between *Christ in Concrete* and *Three Circles of Light*? What would you consider the . . .

P.D.: Right off the top of my head, the purity. *Christ in Concrete* is pure. The widow is pure. Her son is pure. These are our two protagonists.

M.D.: What made you decide to do a biography of the murderer of Maria Goretti?

P.D.: Well, to begin with, there was a book that preceded it. Sophia Loren . . . I was called in by Fox. What was the name of the company? Fox . . . I thought there were two names, I think.

M.D.: Twentieth Century?

P.D.: Twentieth Century Fox. One of the Skouras brothers, the two of them were the heads of the studio. George Skouras called me and he had a big estate at White Plains or Westchester, N.Y. He said, "I've been told that that's your . . . One of our actresses, Sophia Loren, wants to do the life of this woman, Mother Cabrini, St. Cabrini, and I was told that you're the person who could get the material together." The money was good, and he gave me a contract and I took a couple of months, whatever it was. I forgot how long. And I fell in love with the people in the Cabrini story dearly. This was a real human being, a person. I only love good people. Good people are born. When you meet a good person, a knowledgeable person, an ethical person, he didn't learn it in school or class like that. It was just in his genes, in his blood; his character was there, just like his face and everything else. Then something happened, and they decided not to do it. So here I was with ... I got paid, but I had this marvelous material. So my agent brought it ... well, at that time I had an agent named Jasque Shon Brun who had handled *Peyton Place*. He was well connected. He brought the material to Random House. Random House snapped it up and gave me a contract—this labor of love. And when I was finished with the first draft, they gave me, in a couple of weeks. They gave me a fifty-page critique! I followed every page and the book was perfect! You read it?

M.D.: It's a perfect book.

P.D.: *The Immigrant Saint*. And that was chosen by the four Catholic book clubs. It had a full-page introduction by Cardinal Pizzardo, Secretary of State. You can call him the Vice Pope. *The Penitent* came later. My darling wife, Helen, came to me with a copy of the *New York Times*. I have no consistencies. I don't have an addiction to newspapers and magazines and all that; it's too much. I have to read every issue, you know. To me it seems like a sentence or prison sentence or something. Anyway, she said, "There's a story in the *New York Times*. The church that you used to go to, St. Michael's Monastery in West Hoboken; they're setting up a shrine to this little girl who resisted rape and was killed by a young farmer, etc." I said, "Yeah, that sounds interesting; I'll look into it." So I went there to see the monastery. I went to St. Michael's Monastery. That's the place where I came home with a strawberry shortcake. Remember *Christ in Concrete*? That's the place I went to where they gave me strawberry shortcake. But this time I come back as an author. I didn't remind them of that; I didn't say anything about that. It so happened that there was a nice, middle-aged Irish priest named Father Grierton, a nice-looking man with gray hair, and he had dandruff all over his shoulders. I'll never forget that. And he had just come from many years in Italy, Rome, in the Father General House of the Passionist Fathers. It was right slap ... like across the street was St. Johns Latterana. In the Passionist headquarters was the *Scala Santa*, the stairs which Christ went up to be interrogated by Pilate. The holy people, now, they go up those stairs on their hands and knees. They go up with their shoes off and all that sort of stuff. I met ... he said, "I just come from there." He was familiar with the whole process of the Beatitude and the canonization of Maria Goretti. He knew the whole story and he knew the postulant, Padre Mauro. I have pictures of my kissing Fr. Mauro's hand. I have pictures of ... oh, hell, maybe I think I know where the pictures are, pictures taken by—it's the journalist or the photographer who accompanied me on my research in Italy. I spent the week with Serenelli [the murderer of St. Goretti]. Then the book section of Prentice-Hall. Prentice-Hall made up a beautiful copy for me to give to the Pope. The second time I was with Pope John, I was received differently. There wasn't a felicity; there was something disturbing. Cardinal Pizzardo spoke up. We were talking in Italian. He says to me, "*Ah, figlio mio, mi sembre Christopho scolato* [Ah, my son, you seem to be a Christian scholar] . . . . His Holiness and I, we feel that *La piccolo Goretti non e meritava erasse fata santa*" [The little Saint Goretti did not merit being a saint]. I was shocked. Well, here I write the book, *e perche* [and why?] People don't know the Italian mind; the Italians' Pope mind. We have a family sense of life. *Una famiglia tutta la Christiana* [one Christian family, all of us], the poor boy [Serenelli] was driven by lust because he wrote that he studied, went to school for six months. He knew how to read and he read all these pornographic things—do it or I'll kill you. If she had given in, she would have been alive. Two lives would not have been destroyed and there would have been children; they would be all Catholic. He would have married her. Fortunately he would have married her, and so that was a culmination which I did not write after the book because that would be anticlimax. I wrote it because it was a human story. There was no mythological happening; it was all life as it is.

M.D.: That's great, it's a great book. I enjoyed that.

P.D.: In fact, I ran across some interesting material the other day in my filing cabinet, pictures of what I picked up in Italy—photographs they had made a movie [newspaper publicity]. A crude movie out of . . . They had somebody that looked like him and so forth and so on.

M.D.: OK, I think . . . I could go on all night. I got that ferry to catch. Can you autograph these three books for me?

Pietro DiDonato autographing copies of his books. Photography by Matthew Diomede.

P.D.: Sure, sure, sure. Beautiful copies.

M.D.: And then let me take . . . can I take a shot of you? A few shots. And I will talk to Dr. Montesi [my dissertation advisor at Saint Louis University] when I get back. This is great; I took pictures of my family and everything. I appreciate the time. It's just one of those things you can just go on and on, you know.

P.D.: Yes, take as many pictures as you want.

M.D.: I mean it. I learned a lot from you. I've read three, I haven't finished *Immigrant Saint*, but I'm almost done. I've been busy teaching, you know. I'm going to see how it goes. I was considering the dissertation; I can use this material any way. I thought of another angle which was a creative dissertation where you do your own work. But we're going to see how it goes; if not, I can still use this probably for some article. But I may go with . . . I'm going to discuss it a little more with him [Dr. Montesi], you know, and see what we've got going. Creative dissertation, of course is when you do your own, like a book of poems and all, and I've done like poetry, you know. But I can use it [the material]. I've got to discuss an angle here. I feel so inadequate, because I haven't read the other two there. And then I've got to concentrate on a problem and then work it with the problem. I love the way it turns around at the end [referring to *Christ in Concrete* as he autographs it].

P.D.: Keep your health up; you're [my wife and I] both healthy.

M.D.: See, like the dissertation works with an exact idea of your problems, including the problem you intend to investigate. The bibliography—others who have contributed to your field, historically, philosophically. Describe in detail how you plan on investigating the problem and . . .

P.D.: Well, I'm depending on you for the return of the [unbound xeroxed copy of *This Woman*] . . . That's it; that's all I require. Come and take a look at Geremio on the wall. [We walk from his yard to inside Pietro's home]. . . A picture of him on the wall. In that room and when I was in California, my son took them all down and left a couple of them up.

M.D.: I get so busy teaching, you know. I just got some break, August 1, to get over here and I said I was going to try and get to see you.

P.D.: Well, this is the son that's living with me.

M.D.: Looks like John Travolta, you know.

P.D.: That coffee party . . . He's taking drama coaching.

M.D.: I think I might have talked to him on the phone.

P.D.: Yes, yes, you talked to him and he is delightful. And this is my beautiful Chinese friend, Leona. I don't believe it's so dark in here. Can you see? [We enter the room with pictures on the wall.]

M.D.: I can, I can. That's the cover I have; it's in my room at home. That chair is on the back cover of some of your books.

P.D.: That's a cemetery chair—cemetery chair, a graveyard chair. That was taken by the famous Eve Arnold of Magnum. She's a world-famous

Items on the wall of Pietro DiDonato's home. Photograph by Matthew Diomede.

photographer. And this was taken while I was laying bricks. A Jewish friend named Samuel Levine. He made the camera himself. He was a security guard. He took that and this one here; this is an old shot of me with Norman Mailer at the . . .

M.D.: Long Island?

P.D.: No. At the Tavern on the Green . . . big party, big party for Mario Cuomo [then governor of New York] of Mario Cuomo's book and all that. Cuomo said to me, "Don't read this; this is not literature"—that's my father, just before he was killed . . .

M.D.: Good Friday.

P.D.: He [Helen's father] was killed on Armistice Day, and he died on Armistice Day, Helen's father . . .

M.D.: Good Friday, that magic day.

P.D.: This is *Christ in Concrete* in German. It's in eighteen languages. Here's my darling, darling, oh, I miss her [pointing to her picture].

M.D.: She's a beautiful lady.

P.D.: Oh, God, she was beautiful! A prize like pearls. Wonderful, wonderful woman! This is what I wrote about. You'll read it in this one. *This Woman*. There's no bullshit in that. I took a little liberty here or there. [Pointing to a translated German edition of *This Woman*.] So I have a . . . then of course I own the . . . my son called me, he said, "Dad, get the current *Life* magazine—this is my work." In vitro he's got . . . What is this? Oh, he just wanted me to see it. My Peter does all this [pictures of in vitro fertilization].

M.D.: The photography?

P.D.: No, no, no, he does . . . he takes the eggs out of the woman and . . .

M.D.: Yeah, the gynecologist. Yeah, yeah.

P.D.: . . . in a test tube. He gets the embryo in a test tube and puts it back into the woman's womb.

M.D.: Which son was that now?

P.D.: He is three years older than this guy.

M.D.: OK, that's the older one, Pietro.

P.D.: Pietro. He has a beautiful eleven-year-old daughter, Francesca, and a six-year-old boy, Rafael.

M.D.: That's great!

P.D.: So last night the local chemist, Three Village [Stony Brook, New York] chemist, Mike Diandro? He was an Italian-American. He brought it [the issue of *Life* magazine] over and I fed him clams and spaghetti and she does the clams. Garbina, Garbina [pointing to a woman helper].

M.D.: My father's done a lot of that [clamming]. Take care [saying goodbye to Garbina in the kitchen].

P.D.: You've got plenty of stuff. You came all the way here so you deserve a lot of stuff.

M.D.: Well, I'll tell you, you're really generous, I'll tell you that much. You've got that Italian generosity. I'm going to leave the book and the address and I'll try to get that [your copy of *This Woman*]. . . you know I'll get that back to you, not try; I'll get it back to you.

P.D.: I'll carry it [the xeroxed copy of *This Woman*] over for you [walking to my car and to my waiting family].

M.D.: You got all of that.

P.D.: [After he meets my family] I married Helen. He [another person] met Helen before I married her, and after I had married her, he said if I had met her before, I would have married her. He married Ginger Rogers' niece and the wedding was held at Gypsy Rose Lee's town house in New York City.

B.D.: Oh, how wonderful.

P.D.: And then I was tormented, that crazy Catholic in me—you know, my wife—she met some other guy for ten years. I crucified her, especially when I got drunk. And so then Bennett Cerf said to me [referring to *This Woman*], "Pete, write the book." So I wrote the book and then when I finished it, he said, "Pete, Helen has to sign a release. I can't publish the book without a release from her. She was so special. She could sue the hell out of me." So we set it [a meeting] up in a hotel, Central Park West, for a couple of days. She cried, she was insulted, I denigrated her past, I besmirched her husband . . . I was ready to break up. So he said, "We'll put it on the shelf." Sykes Cummings, the great, great editor—he used to edit Truman Capote. I met all these people: Sinclair Lewis, John O'Hara, Eugene O'Neill. I met all

APPENDIX A

Pietro DiDonato and the author's family. Left to right: his wife, Barbara; his mother, Josephine; his father, Frank; Pietro DiDonato. Photograph by Matthew Diomede.

these creatures up there. The whole week we spent together. He [Bennett Cerf] had a nephew named E. N. Ballantine, an English Jewish nephew, and his American wife, Betty, and they opened up a publishing house called Ballantine Press. So he [Bennett Cerf] said, "I'll tell you what," he said; "I don't want to take a chance being sued by Helen, God knows better than you." I turn it over to them, Ballantine Press. It came out from Ballantine Press. Then he [Cerf] turned around and he bought Ballantine Press.

M.D.: Could you tell my wife about your son [his oldest son], Pietro?
B.D.: Yes.
M.D.: Oh, yeah, yeah. *Life* magazine has an interesting event, in vitro fertilization.
P.D.: In-vitro, and he . . .
M.D.: So you got to get a copy of that . . . gynecologist.
P.D.: He was tops . . .
M.D.: Where is he?
P.D.: At San Jose, California. You lived in California?
B.D.: Yeah, I used to live in San Francisco for a little while.
P.D.: I loved San Francisco.
B.D.: Go back every chance I get.
P.D.: [Talking to my father:] *Stato a San Francisco?* [Have you been in San Francisco?]

M.D.: No, but San Pedro.

F.D.: Yeah, San Pedro, I got my niece, my nephews in San Pedro, but I have never been there.

P.D.: It's like Italy. [To my father:] *Tu ha la face di California* [You have the face of California].

F.D.: I have not been to California.

M.D.: He hasn't gone to Florida; he wanted . . . he wants to go to Florida, too, you know.

P.D.: Well, I lived . . . I couldn't stand Florida. Oh, my God!

B.D.: It's so beautiful.

P.D.: I lived in Lauderdale-by-the-Sea; I lived in Pompano, I built a beautiful, beautiful home in Lauderdale-by-the-Sea, and we were having a marvelous time. I couldn't breathe, I couldn't breathe. My wife she . . . it didn't bother her. Over in Venice.

M.D.: Like Barbara [my wife], nothing bothers her. She could live anywhere.

P.D.: I like your face [my wife's].

B.D.: We got something in common here.

P.D.: We're all four good-looking people here, five! The best-looking ones. *La regina!* [Pointing to my mother:] The queen!

J.D.: Yeah.

M.D.: Listen, this has been fun.

B.D.: We'll see that it [the manuscripts] gets back to you safely; it'll come like Federal Express. Wonderful.

M.D.: Take care; thanks a lot. Listen, thanks a lot. Thanks a lot for the time and everything.

P.D.: Good, good. Do good work; you've got good material there. You've got good material. Assimilate it.

M.D.: And I was telling you about the choice whether to go with the creative dissertation.

P.D.: Somehow you can do it more than one way. Just don't do one . . . you do it this way, do it that way, do it this way and exploit it for all it's worth. You've got many outlets.

M.D.: Thanks a lot.

P.D.: Because I don't imitate anybody. I mean, you know there's only one DiDonato.

B.D.: Yeah, that's right.

P.D.: You can't say he likes this one or likes that one and so on. In fact, *la prima volta ma trova Italia* [the first time I saw Italy] I was a guest of a film producer, Franco Rossi. *Vicina Piazza di Spania,* on top of the stairs there and he had a big party. There were *tutti grandi del cinema e communiste e compagnanni.* [There were all these famous people of the film world and Communists and their companions].

F.D.: Rosselini, Rosselini?

P.D.: Yeah, yes, yes. *Rossellini voleva fa* [wanted to] . . . I know, Rossellini wanted to make my movie, and I think that an American, Eddie Dmytryk. I didn't like that fellow and I never did like him. Anyway, Fellini, big tall fellow, in a low voice. He was saying to . . . I heard him talking to Franco Rossi. He said, "*Questa DiDonato che parla Turco?" Io parleva il dialecto di Vasto?* [I guess I was speaking the dialect of Vastese. Rossi said, "Does DiDonato talk Turkish?"]

M.D.: Yeah, we get stepped on when we are not treated so well.

P.D.: And I do it deliberately; I rub it in.

F.D.: It's funny, yeah; people from the north [of Italy] don't understand the south. I was in the Italian navy, you know, and they mixed it.

P.D.: Al Italia! Al Italia!

F.D.: Al Italia!

M.D.: Isn't that something? It's amazing. You've got the north/south split.

F.D.: I was in the Navy, you know there was peacetime, too. Two years in Venice. See, I was the toughest, I wasn't going anywhere, I read about books, you know. Like it was a curse [not to travel by sea], he said, "Yeah, you want to go to sea; you are going to stay here. Two years in Venice! I know Venice better than New York. On account of the classification. You know when you go in the Navy they ask you and I told them *Ferraio* [blacksmith]. *Mi dannero perche . . . le fanna voluntari che la scola dimechanci. Quandovai diurno non dava and mi dattero-* [I told them I was a mechanic and went to school for that and they assigned me to shoot torpedoes, instead.]—you got to serve! *Torpediera!* What the heck, I am going to shoot torpedoes?

P.D.: I tell you, oh, boy, I could keep you all laughing. The sense of humor of the Italians is . . .

F.D.: I was in Italy, you know, for a month. I still have my sister there, and my *cugina la* [my cousin, there]. And I was surprised, I was surprised that the kids they talk real Italian. You know, mother and father when they argue, they talk dialect—Italian. When they talk to the children, they talk the real Italian . . .

P.D.: Yes, I know. Yes, yes, I know, I know. Even in Vasto, when I go there the kids say, "*Questo parla la lingua antigua—*" Vastese, the ancient Vastese, a dialect [This man speaks ancient Vastese]. Sure, that's what I heard at home.

F.D.: It shouldn't be that way. One language! Not so many dialects!

P.D.: But then a lot of northerners, they came down to live in the south. You know they brought machinery and this and that and everything else and modern life. Italy is very sophisticated, very sophisticated.

F.D.: They're not sleeping down there any more [referring to the south].

P.D.: *L'ultima volta io stato a la è ditta l'una figliola, ma che parla da America?* [Last time I was in Italy, a young woman said to me, "Who speaks of America today?"] She says you live in the twentieth century. In Italy we live in the twenty-first century!

M.D.: That sounds good.

P.D.: That's true; I love Italy.

F.D.: No more *alphabeta* [the alphabet]; years ago, whoever went to high school had to be the son of a *Padrone* [a rich landowner]. No more now!

P.D.: *I Communisti è ciambatta tutti cosi a la.* [The Communists have changed a lot of things there]. There's a woman present; I can't tell you the graffiti I've read on the walls there. Oh, boy! Sure, sure, sure. *Contra ai Padrone; O contra al Papa!* [Against the Padrone and against the Pope!].

F.D.: Like this *Padrone,* rich people. They've never worked in their life. How the heck do they have so much land? And then they rent the land.

P.D.: I know, I know.

F.D.: Not only that, they [the tenement farmers] pay rent and then the very first fruit they're going to bring it to the *Padrone*. What the hell!

P.D.: Feudalism. Feudalism. It's all gone. Very sophisticated, very sophisticated. I love Italy, I love Italy.

B.D.: I can tell.

M.D.: Yeah.

P.D.: *Io parlavo con Fellini, a famoso rigista di cinema vicina piazza* [I was talking to Fellini, a famous movie director, in the square], a bunch of Buddhist Americans, you know, with the strap on the face. We were talking to *alla contandina che vendeva a fiori ha vista di meccanicie ditte si Columbus ha fate fati i cazzi sui!* . . . [a merchant who was selling flowers, and he saw these Buddhists and he said if Columbus would only have minded his own Goddamn business!] He said, the Americans, they brought us drugs and rags. All the Americans came over and brought their rags and the drugs and so on. I tell you the Italians, oh, boy, they're smart. But their television is beautiful, the machinery, the cars, the buses, the trains . . .

M.D.: I got students from Aer Italia. Aer Italia; they study aviation engineering in St. Louis and I've given them help. They've been over to my house. In fact, Dr. Montesi bought the tables and picnic table with the Italian flag up on top and we had them over . . .

B.D.: At his house.

M.D.: Yes, at his house, and he invited some faculty over . . .

P.D.: Will you see him when you go back? Oh . . .

M.D.: Yes, yes, I'll see him.

P.D.: Give him my regards! I don't know where we're going to hold the next convention AIHA [American-Italian Historical Association]. Every year it's at a different place. Last year was at San Francisco.

B.D.: Yes.

M.D.: Yes.

P.D.: They paid all my expenses and then when I got to the hotel there were no single rooms, so they gave me a suite. I had a suite all to myself.

M.D.: Really, great, great.

B.D.: Wonderful. Wonderful. Very nice.

P.D.: I bawled the hell out of them, too. I said, "You're discovering me now, huh?" I said all the Jews know me. All the Jews read my books. It's true, because the Jews read books.
B.D.: Yes, sure.
M.D.: Yes, yes. Take care. Thanks a lot.
P.D.: Beautiful, beautiful. *Allora, tanto amore* [Then all my love to you].
F.D.: *Arrivederci; tante cose* [Goodbye—so many bountiful things to you].
B.D.: Take care. Wonderful meeting you. Take care.
M.D.: Thank you very much for your time.
P.D.: You know I'm here. I mean it.
M.D.: OK, thank you very much.
B.D.: OK, we'll keep in touch; we'll let you know how it goes. And we'll get these things back to you by Federal Express or something so to make sure that you get them.
P.D.: Yes, yes, yes.
M.D.: She'll take care of it.
P.D.: I mean, don't break your neck doing it, but as long as I get it back. I've lost so many beautiful books like you have there. Of course, in those days I was drinking and when I was drunk, I'd give away everything. Here, take it, take it, take it. But I don't drink any more; I stop drinking.
B.D.: You look good.
P.D.: Five years ago.
B.D.: You look good. I know you told me about your heart operation, but you look good.
P.D.: Yes, yes. I have good days and bad days, you know. Eighty years old, after all, huh?
M.D.: Yes.
B.D.: You don't look it.
M.D.: Yes.
F.D.: You take Geritol?
P.D.: [All five of us laughing hysterically] No. Ha! Ha! Ha! No, *abbraciata ti da figlia bella ogni tando è medicina*. [No, to be hugged by a beautiful girl very once in a while is my medicine].
M.D.: Thank you very much, OK? Take care.
B.D.: See you again, stay well.
M.D.: Thank you very much, OK?
P.D.: Bring everybody back safely.
M.D.: Yes, good enough.

Pietro DiDonato standing by the concrete wall that he built. Photograph by Matthew Diomede.

APPENDIX B

Personal Interview, 8 August 1991

PARTICIPANTS:

P.D.: Pietro DiDonato
M.D.: Matt Diomede
F.D.: Frank Diomede, the author's eighty-five-year-old father

DiDonato and I began by discussing writing and real writers and what makes them write as we started the interview. This is where we begin our interview.

P.D.: "Real writers," he said. "What real writers? Why do you write? What's your objective?"
M.D.: Yes, yes . . .
P.D.: Most of them write for money, fame, or this and that. I write like a missionary.
M.D.: Yes.
P.D.: I got a hard-on for the world, for the injustice and for the insanity. This Iraq suit, this hero stuff and all that. They are all murderers. These robots went over there to kill little kids and all that. We go by the result of an action. This road to hell is really paved with good intentions. Look at it, look at it! Look at the results. Thousands or more sick and crying every day from cholera, from diarrhea, from need. Oh, Christ Almighty!
M.D.: See, one of the questions I had: there are some wonderful, wonderful phrases you mentioned in my last interview [see pp. 19–21 in this volume]. I don't know if you want to take any of them and possibly trace the development of the concept in some of our works. One of them was, I think, "I am a protestor," with a sense of "rebellion." There was another one, that love can shame death. No matter what we do it takes place in mystery. Love results from this sacredness. And then you spoke about victimization—how the victim does not rebel. And you had a wonderful quote last time. These are some of the concepts that I'm tracing in your works. "The only God I

have now is beauty and my wife." Those are beautiful statements that you can see develop throughout some of your work.

P.D.: Absolutely! Well, it's a contrast to the blindness, the amorphousness of the concepts of people. What do I mean by that? Where's the mother, where's the father, where's the personalization? . . . the private times? . . . where is it? They are running down the flesh. The flesh is sacred. You know the flesh is sacred when something goes wrong with your body. Where do you think the soul is? It's in the brain; it's in consciousness.

M.D.: The soul plays an important part in *This Woman*.

P.D.: Yes, yes, yes.

M.D.: The horned satyr and the Christian soul.

P.D.: Sure, and the only defense you've got against death is love. If you don't have love in your home, in your work, in your surroundings, you're in hell. And I don't mean the love of this fairy guinea, you know: hug me, hug you—what's his name? Oh, I met him; Oh, my God! Mario Cuomo [governor of New York] introduced him to me. About real people, what I'm talking about breaks down, specifically, to communication. You don't go by what people say; you go by what people do. They talk nice and this and that and the other. Hitler talked nice. Uh, uh, truth, love, this and that, and everything else, and mass murder . . . The lies!

M.D.: Where did the title *This Woman* come from?

P.D.: Do you take this woman to be your lovely wedded wife? Do you take this man—this woman, this man.

M.D.: Could *This Woman* be named partially for Grazia LaCafone in *Three Circles*? Since you refer to her as "this woman" after she banishes Stella and shatters Paul's BB gun? That phrase was so conspicuous.

P.D.: I don't remember that, but . . .

M.D.: *Qualla donna,* you know?

P.D.: Yeah, yeah.

M.D.: Stella.

P.D.: Yeah, it could be used in many different ways. I have been . . . we're all conditioned. There are two factors: heredity and then searching for answers. I was a bright kid. I showed you pictures when I was a twelve-year-old. You can see in that kid's face that he was a good kid. He was questioning; he was looking for beauty and then, let me put it this way: you take a normal, bright, passionate, beauty-loving, truth-loving kid; if he tells stories he tells you it's a story. He tells you. He puts his mask on and says, "I'm going to be a bad guy. I'm going to be a good guy." And this is not new; this was done by the Romans in their early life. You take that kid—full of dreams, full of venture, interested in girls—what they smell like, what they taste like, this and that, and everything else—and then kill his father at the age of twelve and then he has to take his father's place. He has to be a husband to his mother; he has to be a father to his brothers and sisters. He has no adolescence, no boyhood. You know that he is going to be indelibly, indelibly affected with the most responsible, profound, paternal sense—an almost godlike paternal sense—of responsibility for his little brothers and sisters. And then he, even today, when I am at the supermarket or in public, I love those kids—even ugly little kids. His mother is ugly and funny. The kid's ugly, but the kid looks at you like a bird, as if to say, "What kind of guy is he? Is he for real? Is he a good guy? Is he a nice guy, or is he a bad guy?" And I never outgrew that, because it was hammered. What do you think I dream about at night? I dream about I'm a bricklayer. What, am I laying bricks? I'm laying bricks with my kid brothers and sisters, so forth and so on. That distinguishes me from the Puzos and the Robert DeNiros. They're playacting, and they're trying to make believe that it is real. I'm real, but playact. They say, "He's a genius. Look how lyrical this and that." No, he suffered, he suffered, he suffered. Why does Dostoyevsky hit home? Where does he get you where the other guys can't get you? But it's all facade. Dostoyevsky was in Siberia. Dostoyevsky was lined up to be shot. And the last moment, saved because the Czar did it on purpose. But he [Dostoyevsky] didn't know that, but the suffering was real. The suffering was real suffering amongst murderers, incestuous murderers. But he found sparks of humanity.

M.D.: Would you say, when you compare *Christ in Concrete* to *This Woman*, what was the reaction to *This Woman* when it was published? Qualitatively, how do you?

P.D.: I know what you're saying. I know what you're saying.

M.D.: Qualitatively, which do you think—what do you think of both works qualitatively?

P.D.: Well, I have a scene in my play [he referred to a drama version of *This Woman*], just one moment. He comes out on the bare stage he rents.... It came to me when I was in Rome. It was during Holy Week, and I went into—on the Via. I went into sort of like a small cathedral. I went in there; the lights were on and everything else, and it was wintertime, around Christmas time—nobody around. And I went up on the altar, and all of a sudden I felt like a celebrant, like a priest. And I imaginatively addressed and imagined an audience there. Then later I transfigured that into a theater on paper, and I got my wife, my mother, my stepdaughter, my wife's mother-in-law from the first husband, and all that. It's . . . some day I'll sell you a copy of the play. The play is really . . . 'cause, see, a play can be superior to a novel. A novel is explained, but a play is the action and the action that lives it. A book you celebrated, you imagined this and that, but when it's live before your eyes then you have to shit or get off the pot. So he calls himself Peter Damiani. Now you know Peter Damiani is one of the fathers of the church back in about the twelfth century.

M.D.: Yes, Peter Damian.

P.D.: Yes, Peter Damian. And he assembles this common spy's wife. And his mother-in-law was hard of hearing. He assembles some actors and actresses like Pirandello's *Six Characters in Search of an Author*. And he says,

"Mrs. So-and-so, you're going to play the spiritualist. Remember Mrs. Miller, his bedroom, and you're going to play this in your bed." He calls the boy and then he says, "You're going to play me, eight-to-twelve." The boy says, "No, I don't want it." "He's not paying you." He said, "I don't want to grow up to be you." It's the guilt. It's what's going on inside of him. It's me; I turned out to be an awful bastard. The saint becomes a devil. Now we can become a saint again some day—stop drinking, smoking. And he [his autobiographical character, Paul] changed his philosophies, too. Then he can come back to being a saint, then he can become his own god. He began to adore his wife who is dead instead of some fucking Jew that he never saw, a God who commits these terrible tragedies. So you see, I got an objective; I'm out to destroy false Gods and so on.

M.D.: Michael Esposito feels that most of your later work suffers a qualitative drop after the success of *Christ in Concrete*. Do you believe this?

P.D.: Yeah. Sure, sure, sure.

M.D.: Esposito says that you say *This Woman* is an obsessive novel about yourself and your wife. It has a complete style of its own. You keep seeing her past. Esposito quotes the D'Alessandro article in the *Italo-American Times*. Isn't *This Woman* more than an obsessive novel?

P.D.: Oh, yes, of course, it's more. It's perennial; it harkens back to Genesis. I'm a jealous God; thou shalt have no Gods beside me. That man has been destined, the male role, and that's why woman has to be denigrated right from Genesis, and I resent that. I resent it in myself. I resent that in society. So you see . . .

M.D.: Do you think that *This Woman* has been properly placed in the corpus of your literature?

P.D.: No, it's ahead of its time. My objective in dramatizing it is that I want the men and women in the audience [the listeners or readers], when they go home, to kill each other. I want them to direct the callings [to direct their own lives with energy and zest] and say, "Yeah, you told me that the first time you ever loved, you enjoyed it. You said, 'Love, it's lust, it's not love.' Boom! Trouble maker!" Because I had . . . this went on inside of me. Of course, when you get to be ninety years old and you're falling apart and dying, those things don't happen. The question is the time, the place, but it does the damage, particularly in our world today. How many women and men you meet have been married once, twice, three times and so forth and so on. Their minds are all soiled, all soiled. They smell bad; these are real sufferings.

M.D.: And the ending of *This Woman* . . . from the beach?

P.D.: Well, the creation of life. But in the play, the play, the degradation and the realization that we're the victim of . . . even now I'm eighty, I was on the phone. You can imagine who I was talking to. A surrogate married woman who comes here and she jumps in bed with me. She's a good grandmother; she's fifty-five. She's a seamstress. She's got a body better than a younger girl.

The fucking animal in us. At least I'm no hypocrite. Can the lion need grass and eat meat? I wrestle with the great Job. I immortalize that in *Christ in Concrete*. Like Job, like Job, like Job. I wrestle with the churches. I wrestle with academia—all authority. They're all full of shit! They're all self-serving; they're all liars. Me first, me first, me first. They're all cruel, and yet there aren't good people doing it.

M.D.: Isn't there a message also at the end of *This Woman*?

P.D.: Well, the book, the book, the ending.

M.D.: Novel?

P.D.: The novel, yes. Birth is a glorious thing, especially if you love the woman. That is wonderful. It's a love child and it's a . . .

M.D.: There is the change, isn't there?

P.D.: It's a step up on the . . . a step in the path, in the illusive . . . path of immortality. Can you imagine that this child was going to be you, or carry your accomplishments, the relay race?

M.D.: Isn't that a fulfillment of Annunziata's prediction in *Christ in Concrete*, "the flower of womankind?" (311).

P.D.: Hail Mary, full of grace, blessed is the fruit of thy womb. For every good woman that child brings out is blessed fruit of her love for the male, *il padrone*, the master; the planter.

M.D.: Is there any relationship to that and Paul's dealing with the past?

P.D.: It's up to you. You are the diviner of the ceremonies. What you put down, don't stick . . . let what I tell you be the soil and so forth. It's how you nourish that with your imagination. It's how many meanings can you give it. You have to intuit, to use your intuition. That's when your life is so successful. But just don't be a xerox, a copier; be an interpreter, an analyzer as a diviner. As a boy I looked like a handmaid, who's not an invoker, who's not a planter, who's not the seminal, but he [the boy becomes the father of a family—he grows and matures] is in *This Woman*.

M.D.: Michael Esposito attributed your excess drinking to dissatisfaction with having to work back at construction since you have felt let down.

P.D.: There's a lot of truth; there's a lot of truth in a lot of things. But there are truths behind those truths. So this way, just use your imagination. See, you have to say what you really feel; how you see it.

M.D.: Whom do you consider the evil person? When I was reading "The Gospels"—psychologically, what characterizes the evil person for you?

P.D.: The liars. The liars. For instance, amongst the Jews, Satan, the father of lies. Because if you tell the truth, forewarned is forearmed, but it is the bastard that lies, whether you lie to yourself or whether you lie to others, or you believe somebody else's lies. That's the road to sure tragedy, to disaster, to evil.

M.D.: On pages 306–11, in *Christ in Concrete*, your mom forgives you and tells the others in your family to follow you. Is this real or is this a dream of hers? Bauer . . . I think, seems to say that your mother is dreaming.

P.D.: Well, that happened, but I don't . . . you see I end it there. I don't say that my mother kept on living, then died of cancer, but I didn't know what to say after that. I shut my vault.

M.D.: Would you call *The Love of Annunziata* a tragedy or comedy?

P.D.: Well, it's not a comedy. It was a tragedy. When we all suffer a loved one, that is tragic. And losing money, that seems tragic. You can lose a leg, lose an ankle—that's not tragic. But when the one you love disappears from the face of the earth, Jesus Christ! You can't forgive this so-called god, but it's pathetic, it's pathetic. Because if you only had a god that you could attack. It's a man—all liars, liars, priests, and Jehovah's Witnesses and Bible thumpers. You see them on television and so forth. When a priest—I never met the Polack. I met two popes. I met Pope John and then Pope Paul. Pope Paul was a nervous wreck. He had problems. He's only a man. How can a man put on those clothes and all that and sit there and talk about God? Has he seen God? What's he talking about? And then the other guy believes in some other god. Liars.

M.D.: In *Christ in Concrete* there are dreams of Geremio as a clown awakening to the words, "I am cheated." In *The Love of Annunziata*, Geremio describes himself as a buffoon. Could you say why you characterized Geremio as a clown or a buffoon in certain parts of your works?

P.D.: He's telling, basically he's telling his wife, Annunziata, that. Because he has a feeling that in the face of death and in the shenanigans and monkey shines he says, that's not me. When it comes right down to the edge of the grave, the Bible says the house of mourning is better than the house of laughter. You know what that means. It's serious, it's true, it's real. People laugh at their own kind of crazy things. Just like parties; everybody's having fun. Ha, ha, ha! Drinking, drinking, ha, ha, ha! Every sidewalker would say, "Jesus Christ, I can't pay the mortgage; can you loan me a thousand dollars?" Yeah. There go the friendships [the friends would be hesitant to lend the money]; I thought the friendships were alive.

M.D.: Yeah. In a number of your works the imagery of the theater is mentioned. In *This Woman* Paolo says, "A theater: life is a theater with no exit." And the gospel of redemption occurs in the theater. In *The Love of Annunziata*, Geremio comes alive in Annunziata's mind in scene three. Why do you favor the use of the image of the theater? What role does the theater play, especially in *This Woman*? I've taken it from different angles.

P.D.: I was reading something very significant about Dostoyevsky. He said, and one of his characters says, "In the beginning man was an actor." And then religion can hurt him. If you study yourself and your behavior and company, you're playing a part. Every part is responsible. Like Delmore Schwartz; you've heard of him?

M.D.: Yes.

P.D.: He wrote one great short story. I think it was called, "In Dreams They're Our Responsibilities." With dreams come responsibilities, and that's true. All the equivalents, or in your own words, and you can transpose that and say which I wrote yesterday—commitments are strange things. You know, I love you, but the marriage is turning . . . I promise; I'll sign a contract. That's why they're [forced promises/commitments] dead. So many times people are better off by not being married legally or anything like that. By living together until they prove that they love each other, and so forth. And not have kids until they prove that they love each other. Because that's when all our heartbreak comes. Oh, he betrayed me; he lied to me, this and that; he left me and this and that. You said you loved me and . . . Oh, my God!

M.D.: In *The Love of Annunziata*, Annunziata imagines Geremio has returned as a stranger and ashamed. And in *Christ in Concrete*, a father is dreamed of by Paul. The father is ashamed and a stranger. Why do you choose these two words in these books and in other works? A stranger and ashamed.

P.D.: I don't know. But when my darling [his wife, Helen] died, I was ashamed for not committing suicide with her. I let her die. I didn't have the courage to go with her. Here I am alive. The only thing I can say is when I'm doing it or after I do it, forgive me, Helen, forgive me.

M.D.: What do your mother and father represent in your life and in the corpus of your literature?

P.D.: In my case, I loved. It was a conspiracy. Real love is a conspiracy. Even when he would beat the shit out of me, I deserved it. My mother, too . . . I felt better after he beat the shit out of me. I really did. I was wrong. I was wrong. I was a liar; I wouldn't lie; he beat me!

M.D.: Why do you call *Three Circles of Light* the *Three Circles of Light*? Does it come from . . . I traced it to Dante's *Paradiso*. Is it canto 33? [Dante sees a light containing three circles that brings him to understand that God's love moves the sun and the stars.]

P.D.: Yes, yes. Well, that was a particular genius on his part because, suppose, for example, when you see the movies *Jesus Christ* and all that, he looks like some fucking fag that just came out of a beauty parlor. Weak face and all that. You cannot, you cannot, take a man's face and portray it as God. The sun, the splendor of the heavens, the stars. Because a man shits, a man pisses, a man stinks, a man smells. You can't depend on a man. A woman, perhaps, yes. So it was a bit of a genius there. Of course he meets Beatrice there; he meets this one and that: Virgil, Santa Lucia and so forth. Do you notice that the Jews intimate a little bit of that when on the top of Mount Sinai, Jehovah does not appear to Moses to give him the commandments in the image of a human being—the burning bush? I remember. That's why we should burn this bush. Must be God that burned.

M.D.: I also noticed the word "circles" is mentioned three times when you and your mother go to trace your father's movement with Delia Dunn and three circles down by the house where she was. The word "circles" is mentioned three times, OK? And you catch him going in three circles.

P.D.: I don't remember. I don't remember.

M.D.: Yes, yes. I thought it was interesting how it came up.

P.D.: Of course the circle was the perfect form—perfect form. Planets are slender. And then the colors and then the light, three circles of light.

M.D.: There's another question that I had on that . . .

P.D.: So you can use your imagination.

M.D.: But what do stars play in your works? Especially in *This Woman*. Yeah, the stars were in there. Does the concept of home mean something at all in your works? I'm reminded of *The Odyssey* or William Saroyan's *Human Comedy* here. Is there any connection with your choosing a Mr. Saroyan as the coffee-and-nut-store owner in your seemingly universal concept of Paul or Geremio returning home?

P.D.: Where is that, *Three Circles*?

M.D.: I think home in *The Love of Annunziata*. He comes home. There's a constant returning to home in *Christ in Concrete*. *Three Circles*, I guess, coming home.

P.D.: Coming back to the womb or coming back to . . . it's not a home if there is not a woman in it. If there is not a woman, there is not a home.

M.D.: And that's related to Annunziata. She had a lot to do.

P.D.: Oh, sure. A woman is the home. I lived in and out of the house, not in the home. I expected Helen to consider the door.

M.D.: So what you say is very important. A woman is very important to the corpus of your literature?

P.D.: Oh, sure, absolutely. A woman is the altar and the home. Yeah.

M.D.: Yeah. A satyr appears in *This Woman* and it appears in *Three Circles*. In *Three Circles* it appeared in the masonry of Pellegrini's drugstore.

P.D.: Satyr?

M.D.: Yeah, satyr. What meaning does the satyr play in your work? The end of *This Woman*, too, with the Christian soul.

P.D.: There's another word . . . what did I call it?

M.D.: The behorned satyr?

P.D.: No, no . . . or was it the . . . what was the other word? [searching for another word for satyr].

M.D.: I know what you're getting at.

P.D.: Well, it happened, it happened to be that . . . it's still there, it's still there. The old building is still there.

M.D.: We should take a picture of it.

P.D.: I had a picture of it and I may have a copy of it somewhere of *Coronet*.[1] I don't know whether you remember? And I did a fabulous documentary called, "My Hoboken, My People." I can give you a copy of that poster.

M.D.: Sounds interesting. Sounds interesting.

P.D.: Yes, and there's about a dozen photos by a very famous photographer, Eve Arnold. Gertrude Berg, you know, Molly Goldberg [an actress, later on television; this is her stage name], on the radio. She got me a . . . she was my friend, she got me a. . . . There's another word [for satyr].

M.D.: Half and half [a description of the satyr, half horse and half human, that appears at the end of *Three Circles of Light* (246)]?

P.D.: Yes, yes, yes. Let me go get it. I think I have an extra copy [of the advertisement of the article for *Coronet*].

M.D.: Yes, OK.

P.D.: [Reading the back of the advertisement of *Coronet* where handwriting appears.] "Vultures, wisdom and big wives of yours, Gypsy queen woman faces the ages [sic] truth of a woman. *Laputanna Americana*, reptile leaves, bombs." Oh, shit, I can't give you this one. [These appear to be DiDonato's scrap copy of some other manuscript of his.]

M.D.: No, you can't give me that, that's right. It's got . . .

P.D.: I got another one.

M.D.: *Three Circles* is in there, plus a couple of other ones?

P.D.: This is 'way, 'way back. 'Way, 'way back.

M.D.: That's interesting what you got.

P.D.: Let me see the other copy. Let me see . . . I didn't know this [there was writing on the back copy of the advertisement of his article on Hoboken, N.J., in *Coronet*] until I went like this and turned it over. [Reading the back of the copy.] Roman Marie.

M.D.: Yes. That's great!

P.D.: Two hundred thirty-seven East Fifth Street.

M.D.: Yes, yes, this is interesting.

P.D.: Marie Marchand [some woman DiDonato apparently jotted down on the back of the *Coronet* advertisement].

M.D.: Rose Mary Marie.

P.D.: Romany, Romany.

P.D.: I wonder what the other one . . .

M.D.: What role does Annina play in this film that at one point she utters a marvelous passage? "Paul . . . do not recognize doubt. . . ." [*This Woman*, 178].

P.D.: Who?

M.D.: "Paul . . . do not recognize doubt, for I now say to you the Truth. Your Soul is. Your Soul will come to you only if you want your Soul. It is simple, and not mysterious nor hidden. To receive it you must desire it" (*This Woman*, 178).

P.D.: Who says that?

M.D.: Annina, I think. Yes. "Awakening, the effulgence of her message left him exalted in momentary beatitude" (*This Woman*, 178). Is that great? Was there a sister Annina in your life?

P.D.: Now, wait; I'll show you something. I'll show you something. I discovered it just a couple of days ago rummaging through boxes. Here's the answer.

M.D.: [Looking at an autographed copy of *Christ in Concrete*] Yes, yes. "To my dear sister, Anne, the most wonderful woman in the world, from brother, Peter, March 19, 1939, Hilltop, Northport." That's great! Yes, yes!

P.D.: She was three years older than I. She was the Mother and I was the Father.

M.D.: Yes. I see, yes. She was the Mother and you were the Father.

P.D.: *Lust Wills Eternity* [title of *This Woman* in the German edition].

M.D.: *Lust Wills Eternity*. Great, great! Here's my dad [looking out the window, seeing my dad arrive to end the interview].

P.D.: Good title. What do you think the waves do? What do you think the sun does? What do you think the volcano does? It has an orgasm? What do you think the fucking gnats and birds and insects—the ninety-ton whale that fucks a sixty-ton little sweetheart—is a must!

M.D.: It's like a cycle.

P.D.: Or the sperm, the sperm that goes up there and fights its way up? I saw a cartoon; one sperm has got a little outboard motor on his ass.

M.D.: You've got the beach scene in that [*This Woman* 220], and then . . .

P.D.: Yes, oh yes. That was real. That was real. That was Crab Meadow Beach.

M.D.: And the beach scene is what Nazone is extremely fond of. The day that he falls, he wants to go to the beach and not go to work (*Christ in Concrete*). You see?

P.D.: That's right.

M.D.: So both of them, the beach scene of Nazone in *Christ in Concrete* and the one in *This Woman* (220), come together?

P.D.: Our whole town lived right on the Adriatic.

M.D.: That's right, yes.

P.D.: Beautiful, oh, beautiful town, and there is a high palisade . . .

M.D.: That's Abruzzi?

P.D.: Vasto.

M.D.: Vasto, yes, Vasto.

P.D.: It was founded before Rome by the Greeks.

M.D.: In *This Woman*, Isa Tromm says to Paul, "Don't think too much about life, honey; live it before you lose it" (76). Would you say this statement characterizes your life? Or does it characterize the life of someone else possibly closer to you?

P.D.: Well, Isa, that's my wife, her name was Helen Mull. And she was a . . . she belonged to . . . she was wise—natural woman, natural wise.

M.D.: So, in *This Woman*, a line of interest appears: "What could the gift of conscious life truly call home?" (159). What is home to you? Can you show how the concept of home plays a part in your works?

P.D.: Home is that woman. If she is in a tent or a cave, skins and furs . . . it's the woman. The woman is like a mother. Mother kept telling me, "Don't worry, don't worry, don't worry about anything." Because if you're cold, she will warm you, or if you're hot, she'll cool you—a real woman.

M.D.: On top of page 164 of *This Woman*, you speak of the love/hate Paul has for Isa Tromm—the all-consuming love. Could you define love?

P.D.: The most substantial concept that I have is that they're androgynous. The other half is there. She's your other half of yourself. You're not complete. You're not complete.

M.D.: On page 176 of *This Woman*, Paul refers to life as the "all-whore life" and "the fabulous prostitute" that permitted Jack Tromm to live. What is your definition of life?

P.D.: What did I say there?

M.D.: "All-whore life; . . . the fabulous prostitute" that permitted Jack Tromm to live. What is your definition of life?

P.D.: That is a very . . . very . . . more than one, more than one definition.

F.D.: Matthew [my father entering the house to tell me it's time to leave].

P.D.: Come on in.

M.D.: He is giving me the signal [to finish the interview].

P.D.: [To my father] Come on in, young fellah.

M.D.: I think we're getting ready to go.

P.D.: There's the young fellah, for God's sakes [my dad is eighty-five]. You're looking good, Frank. You're looking good, you're looking good. *Quanti anni sono*? [How old are you?]

M.D.: I just wanted to . . .

F.D.: We'll wait outside. Who, me? [Humorously.] I stopped counting.

M.D.: *Quanti anni sono*? [How old are you?]

P.D.: Come on. [My father hesitates.]

F.D.: [Born] 1906.

P.D.: [Born] 1906, OK, 1906. I was born in . . .

F.D.: Eighty-five. June, 1906.

P.D.: Eighty-five? . . . I was born in 1911; I'm eighty.

F.D.: Yes

P.D.: 1911?

F.D.: 1911; yes, yes.

P.D.: Five years.

M.D.: He's going strong.

P.D.: You look good. You're nice and slender.

M.D.: OK, we're going to get ready?

F.D.: We'll wait outside.

M.D.: I'll be out in a couple of minutes.

P.D.: Take a lot of basil. Take basil there. Take a lot of basil. Oh, he wants to see the pictures.

M.D.: I'll be out.

P.D.: *Tutti favori* [Help yourself].

M.D.: I want to see if I can get a picture of both of you guys.

P.D.: Yes, yes; outside, inside?

M.D.: OK? Yes, 'cause . . .

P.D.: Where do you take the best pictures . . . outside?

M.D.: Yes, yes.

P.D.: In sunlight?

M.D.: Yes.

P.D.: All right, we will go outside in a couple of minutes.

M.D.: Couple of minutes and I'll get a picture, all right?

P.D.: He's cute.

M.D.: He's all right! So your definition of life?

P.D.: Because, you see, life is really your unlabeled, unnamed true love—true love. And she represents life physically—you can taste life. You see, life is an abstraction—her vagina, her breasts, her armpits, her mouth—this is the nourishment. And now I call it a whore because in life there's death. So this whore makes love to you and destroys you. But, of course, an actor or actress will say, "Well, you know nothing's lost. Your bones and everything else make that fertilizer." I don't go with that—the hell with it! But your so-called God made himself immortal. Make everybody immortal!

M.D.: So the filthy, icy upstate weather of the "Modern City" [where much of *This Woman* takes place]. Is that in Cooperstown? Is that it?

P.D.: Utica, Utica.

M.D.: Utica. OK, that's Utica.

M.D.: And then the Hotel Modern is the . . .

P.D.: Is the Utica Hotel—the Utica Hotel; go ahead.

M.D.: Yes, Utica.

P.D.: Utica Hotel.

M.D.: Utica Hotel. It's not in Massachusetts?

P.D.: No, it's in upstate New York.

M.D.: OK, Utica. And the Skittara, Skittara Cemetery.

P.D.: Oneonta.

M.D.: Oneonta. Yes, yes, I got that.

P.D.: This gives it reality. And you can say that I was up in a conscientious objector camp. But I wanted to disguise everything there.

M.D.: Why do you talk about construction following the cemetery scene when Paolo chops the coffin of Jack Tromm?

P.D.: Let's see. In *This Woman* I'm not an author. No.

M.D.: You're not what?

P.D.: I'm not an author, am I? No.

M.D.: No?

P.D.: I'm not an author. See, I didn't tell the truth but I was a builder, though. I wasn't . . . I omitted. I hadn't looked at *This Woman* in many, many, many years.

M.D.: It's been characterized as a "sexual potboiler" [Esposito, "The

Travail," 56), I think by Esposito, if I'm correct. I refuse to believe that. But I'm editorializing here.

P.D.: Well, you see, Germany was more sophisticated and more thinking like you. It was a big hit in Germany. And they changed the title, though, you know—*Lust Wills Eternity.*

APPENDIX C

A Descriptive Bibliography

Edited and Partially Translated by M. Diomede
from a Personal Interview held 8 August 1991

PARTICIPANTS

    P.M.: Pietro DiDonato
    M.D.: Matt Diomede

The third interview that the author includes here illuminates much of the critical analysis in this book. In order to prepare for a critical examination of DiDonato's works he is following the lead of Edith Heal's book about William Carlos Williams, *I Wanted to Write a Poem* (Boston: Beacon, 1967). In this book Heal attempted to write "a descriptive bibliography of his works including his own account of the writing experience" (v). On 8 August 1991, the author met with Pietro DiDonato at his home in Strongs Neck, Long Island, New York, to attempt a similar project. Mr. DiDonato was asked to talk, with as little interruption as possible, about seven of his works covered in chapters 3 to 9 in this volume. In addition, in the interview he talked about a new unpublished work, "The Gospels."

DiDonato and the author followed the arrangements in the discussion, as listed below:

Chapter 3. *The Immigrant Saint: The Life of Mother Cabrini*, a biography of St. Mother Cabrini.

Chapter 4. *The Penitent*, a biography of St. Sister Maria Goretti.

Chapter 5. "Christ in Plastic," an essay on the assassination of Aldo Moro, Italy's Christian Democrat president.

Chapter 6. *The Love of Annunziata*, a drama.

Chapter 7. *This Woman*, a novel.

Chapter 8. *Christ in Concrete*, a novel.

Chapter 9. *Three Circles of Light*, a novel.

Pietro was asked to specifically mention anything that might help in understanding these works, especially the creation of them. He was also asked to comment on how the works came into being, his overall intention in the works and anything else he might want to add. The following is a presentation of the meeting.

In this section, I asked DiDonato to talk of his seven works and to talk of the creation of them and to add anything he thought might prove helpful to someone analyzing his works. I merely mentioned the title of the work and waited for his reaction.

M.D.: *The Immigrant Saint: The Life of Mother Cabrini.*

P.D.: I was raising money, helping raise money for Boys Town of Italy, founded by Monsignor Calalbini. Among the people that were helping to raise the funds was the wife of one of the owners of the people running the Twentieth Century Fox, the two Greek brothers Byrus and George Skouras . . . But she was Sicilian; her name was Julia, very religious, Julia Skouras; and she called me, and they had an estate up in Westchester, and they were very rich. They called me and said they had Sophia Loren under contract; Sophia Loren wanted to play Mother Cabrini. Of course, Sophia Loren's real name is Cicapelli, and she had been through the Second World War in Naples there and all that. I never really met her. So they gave me a nice big check because they said I was the only one who was qualified to get the material put together for the movie. So three or four months later, when I had all the material, their plans changed, although I had been paid, and I fell in love with Mother Cabrini as a human being. I would never write about a god or saints that I have never seen. I'm not that credulous and naïve. So, realistically, Mother Cabrini did more good for the Italian immigrants than anybody, because prior to her advent the Irish had dominated the parish scene. And my agent brought the material to McGraw-Hill and they immediately gave me a contract to write a book about it, so there I was. It took me about a year, and the book was very successful. Did you see the new copies?

M.D.: No. You told me about that—St. Martin's Press, right?

P.D.: St. Martin's Press.

M.D.: I got the old copies, but . . .

P.D.: Oh, well, so I went to Italy and the places that she founded and built, and it was a happy experience. Now as for *The Penitent*, my wife had read it in the *New York Times*, which is subsequent to that—that the church that I used to go to in West Hoboken, in New Jersey, St. Michael's Monastery which was run by Passionist fathers that were enshrining a part of the skeleton of this little child saint [Goretti], and it would be a shrine there. The story was that two sharecroppers' families [the Gorettis and Serenellis], below the Pontine marshes [of Italy] were working this sharecropping arrangement for an Italian baron. But the environment was dangerous because of malaria and the ground was very rich, though—and they could grow wonderful crops, and they could do better than anyplace else in Italy. And so, the younger man died and there was a widower and his twenty-year-old son,

Alessandro Serenelli. And there was also Luigi Goretti and his four or five kids, and the oldest one was a twelve-year-old girl, Maria Goretti. Luigi died of malaria. After this, the widow said, "We're going back to Ancona" on the east coast, where they came from. She took the husband's place in the field, and the twelve-year-old girl took her place as the mother over everybody—feeding everybody, cooking, and everything. And then the twenty-year-old boy, Alessandro, became sexually passionate about the twelve-year-old girl, Maria, and tried to rape her. He probably would have married her, too. She fought him off and begged him not to do it. She just had gotten her First Holy Communion, so it was not as much a religious story as a human story. And frustrated (he had six months schooling and knew how to read, and he was deep into all these "screw or die" stories), Alessandro tried to kill her and struck her fourteen times with a machete. Before she died (she lived fourteen hours), she forgave him, and so forth, and it was a great story. So I went to St. Michael's Monastery and just by chance one of the Passionist fathers who was involved in the whole process—an Irishman by the name of Father Grierton, had spent many years at the Father General quarters in Rome that was a few paces from St. John the Lateran. In the Passionist place there was the original *Scala Santa*—the stairs that Christ had mounted to see Herod and Pilate. Father Mauro was the postulator of the cause, and I met him through the intercession with the Vatican and the letter to the murderer who had served his full sentence as a minor. Because had he [Serenelli] been one year older, he would have to die in prison, as an adult. There was no capital punishment—there still isn't. If you were twenty-one or more, you never get out, but he was twenty. But he was no stranger to Assunta, the mother of the girl; he was like a son. She was in contact with him during the years he was in prison . . . Because at the trial, when he was condemned, when the trial was held in Regina Coeli [The Queen of Heaven] Temple or Prison which I'd visited—which had formerly been a pagan temple, near the Vatican, on the Tiber River there. When he was there, he got the full sentence of thirty years—three years of solitary confinement and twenty-seven years of hard labor. The judge called Assunta and asked, "What do you have to say?" She stood up before . . . the courtroom was crowded because the child was called a little St. Agnes—the second St. Agnes—the child saint of purity. Rich people were there and the *cognoscenze* [intellectuals]. And it was the advent of the alienists, which today are called psychiatrists. They were alienists in those days. They tried to convince the kid to pretend that he was insane, but he was honest. He said, "No, I killed her; I wanted to rape her." His sexuality was overpowering him, so he got the full sentence. So she said, "I forgive him, like my Maria forgave him," and everybody screamed, "No, no, no, no; hang him!" When they quieted down, she said, "And if our Jesus were here, he would do the same." Everybody broke down and cried, and said, "She should be a saint." This got to be so dramatized. I, then, easily got a contract from Prentice-Hall and a nice advance and expenses and all of that, and I went back that way [to Italy] again and was with her sister, who had been married, the little child Ersilia, who ended up as an elderly woman married to, of all people, a bricklayer. I visited her other sister, who was [now] a nun [Sister Maria Alessandra] in Naples, and I collected all the material and it turned out very good. Naturally, I was with the killer. The reason he permitted me to interview him and stay with him in the monastery of Maciaratta—actually it was Franciscan fathers who lived there. This is where they went to die . . . It was like an old-age place. He had read my book, *Christ in Concrete*, and he had two favorite books, *Delitto e Pena* [*Crime and Punishment* of Dostoyevsky] and *Christ in Concrete* of DiDonato. So we became great friends. We took a lot of pictures together and wept together, and we prayed together and so forth. So that was so rewarding and again I say it had nothing to do with the Jew God named Christ and Jehovah in the Old Testament and all that kind of fatal stuff. It had to do with my people and all truth and humanity. Of course *Christ in Concrete* is not a religious book. It was my father who was killed on Good Friday; they lifted his body out of the wreck and concrete, all that on Easter Sunday, and that was the crucifixion and the resurrection. I wrote the title as an epithet more than as a religious introduction. You see that everything, any work with any intrinsic value has a beginning of genealogy somewhere. It just doesn't spring out from nowhere.

M.D.: "Christ in Plastic" (*Penthouse*, December 1978).

P.D.: The capture of Aldo Moro—the kidnapping and being waylaid and all the policemen and so forth. His being murdered and his being spared and kept in captivity. The purpose of the Red Brigade was to swap him for the leader of the Red Brigade. I forgot his name; I wrote it all down. I got the Officers Press Club Award for it. Bob Guccione called me the day they found Moro's body. Moro's body was found in a little VW station wagon, wrapped up in orange plastic. It had the riddle of bullets and it was right near, right between the headquarters of the Christian Democrats and the Communist Party. They were near each other. Guccione called me and said, "Could you be on the plane out of our J.F.K. [John F. Kennedy Airport, New York] tonight?" He said, "Have your wife go to the bank and take out the three thousand dollars, and I'll have tickets waiting for you at the airport and tomorrow somebody will come out and hand pay you the three thousand dollars to your wife." So I was on the plane that night, and I happened to have several important friends in the Communist Party there. Of course, I didn't know how to approach anybody that was in the Red Brigade. Strangely, on the plane going over, Guccione says, "Pick up a copy of the *New York Times*; there's a lot of information there." When I got to the airport there was no *New York Times* available. And on this big plane (747) in the middle of the aisle there were five or six seats across; there were two young Italians reading the *New York Times*. I said, "Pardon me, when you finish, can I read the *New York Times*?" They said, "Oh, yeah, yeah." It turned out that they were associated with the Red Brigade and they were coming up from Mexico from a place that I knew very well, that I had done a Mexican story on for *Playboy*. San Christobel, Las Casas—very, very historic place, where Cortez stopped and so forth. They had a business in the jungles there—these Italians—of gathering wild orchids, Christ Almighty [with a laugh]! So, when we landed in Rome, they gave me some leads and called up, and little by little I met two actual inside members of the Red Brigade; and they gave me the story—providing I would not tell anybody, because they would lose their necks if they got caught. So it was a very exciting affair, and it came off very well. But the "Christ in Plastic" was not my title. My title was simply *B.R., Brigate Rosso*. But John Lombardi, one of my editors, he says, "*Christ in Concrete*... 'Christ in Plastic?'" So you see, everything has a reason, has a connection.

M.D.: *The Love of Annunziata.*

P.D.: Did you ever see it?

M.D.: No.

P.D.: The book? *American Scenes*? I have it here, see.

M.D.: The book. Yeah, I got that book.

P.D.: And I also have *The Best One-Act Plays*—some nice people brought it to me. They said, "We figure you might not have it right now." What was I getting at? Oh, yeah, yeah, yeah. The Book of the Month Club, you know. I made a lot of money [from *Christ in Concrete*] and my life was transformed overnight. I had access to the environment of the rich people, the movie people and the stage people—and the media world. It revealed to me what kind of people they were, too. I mean meretricious parasites, most of them, and predators and so forth. I was befriended by a famous dance team called "Ray Analdi." There were two great dance teams—Ray Analdi and Tony and Renée Demarco. Mario Analdi married Mary Ray, took me down to Havana with them, where they were dancing at the Copacabana, and they took me backstage with all the nude, beautiful show girls and so forth. And I with them... I ended up in Havana. I then met Hemingway, Meyer Lansky, and all kinds of people at the gambling casino. There was a rich, very rich Italian Neapolitan American named Sylvio Carjulo. He said, "Go to my plantation in the Island Pines. There's a Rolls Royce there, servants and a big boat and everything else," and so I went. He said, "Get away from Hemingway. Don't get drunk with him any more." So when I was there, I decided to make a play out of *Christ in Concrete* and I wrote the first chapter, the first act, and I stopped. When I came back... I was away for almost a year in Cuba. When I came back I knew William Kozlenko. He had a lame leg and he was one of the world's authorities on one-act plays. I then told him I had written the first act and he said, "Let me read it. This is a complete one-act [play], right as it is." So he included it in *American Scenes*, and it was chosen as one of the best one-act plays; that's how that got published. Eventually through the years, I completed the rest of the play. So what else now?

M.D.: *This Woman.*

P.D.: Oh, yes, yes. Well, Ballantine has always been a subsidiary and part of Random House. When the Second World War came, I had protested the Nazi and the Fascist invasion of Spain. I was going to join the Lincoln Brigade, but I had . . . was supporting seven brothers and sisters—all kids. And I didn't have the heart to leave them. So I was very agitated about the American buildup of Fascism and Nazism for the purpose of destroying Russia—this paranoia against the "Red Eagle." And when the War did come, Pearl Harbor and all that, I didn't know I was going to join and I was taking out a girl whose father was an admiral. I introduced her to Ruth Goldberg's family and son, and she married into Jewish money. And her father, who had been a retired admiral, was living in Norfolk, where I was living. He told me to stay out of it. He said, "This war has been fabricated. This is all from the power politics." And then, of course, I was with the general. The army . . . and I visited him on, I think, Governor's Island, where it was, and he said, "Stay out of it." He said, "We professional soldiers don't like what's going on. They're cooking up a war against Russia." I was a pacifist anyway, so I was given status as a conscientious objector, but the Draft Board in Smithtown [New York]. . . . They were so anxious to keep me away from being a conscientious objector; they said, "We'll help you start a little defense industry." I said, "No, shove it! You guys make the war; you fight it." So I ended up in a Quaker camp, in Cooperstown. I was sentimental about James Fenimore Cooper, the first American novelist. A couple of days later, I met my wife, a young widow there, whose father had been killed on Armistice Day in the First World War. You saw the pictures of him. You saw the pictures on the wall, Alexander Dean. D.A.R. and army people and all that. So, all right, getting back to *This Woman*, I've been extremely sensuous and I still am at the age of eighty. In fact, my only God is Venus, and I'm not bragging. I mean it, I mean it. I adore women. In fact, this morning I wrote in my new book, *Lust Wills Eternity*, Love is God and woman is love. Without woman, there would be no world; the rest all is nonsense—all is travesty. She was a widow, and she had been a showgirl and she was from the South from a plantation in Tennessee. A plantation named a "Black Angle." She was a real Cleopatra. You saw the picture up there; she was a beauty, a real beauty—great character, great character. She had a little girl. I pumped her. I asked her [my wife] all kinds of questions. When was the first time you had sex, this and that and everything else. Then she showed me pictures of her husband. He had white hair and blue eyes and . . . old enough to be my grandfather, I guess, and I was contemptuous of all that. I had absorbed all those facts that I should not have found out. Then after, I didn't want to get married; I didn't want any more responsibility. I had raised seven brothers and sisters and a nephew. My mother and all that sort of stuff—my mother had died at only the age of forty-four, of cancer in the uterus. My father was only thirty-six when he was killed. My mother was the same age then. So I left the camp and I went to apply for a transference [sic] to an objective camp in a mental institution called Byberry, outside of Philadelphia. But Helen, she came there and then I transferred to a camp in Maryland, building a canal in the swamp, and she came there, too. She wanted me. She had fallen in love before she met me. Because her husband was a member of the Book of the Month Club and when the famous book *Christ in Concrete* came out with that Byronesque picture of me in the back, she said to the husband, "What do you think of this young Italian?" He said, . . Well, of course he [her husband] was educated; he was a graduate of Union College; he was of Dutch ancestry—"That's an enlightened face." When she saw me in Cooperstown and she recognized me, and that's it. So anyway, after I married her, I kept seeing her with her other husband, in my dreams and everything I did with her. In fact, we were married by my friend Mayor LaGuardia [of New York City]. Julio Picchiarilli, the famous sculptor, who made the Lincoln Memorial in Washington, took him eight years to do it; he was our best man. Then I started to drink, and I became vicious every time I got drunk, and I would try to destroy her past and destroy her. I was a friend of the publisher Bennett Cerf. He was single and he had divorced Sylvia Sidney—that was his first wife. I was telling him that I had married Helen, and he met Helen, and he liked Helen. I kept seeing this other bastard-husband. I kept seeing her in bed with this other guy. He [Cerf] said, "Well, why don't you give me a book on that?" He gave me a contract. That's how *This Woman* got started. When I finished it, Sykes Cummings, the great editor, he and I worked a couple of weeks on it and then it was ready to be published. Bennett Cerf insisted that Helen read it, because he didn't want to be sued. She broke out and cried and didn't want it published. I cried and everything else—he shipped it later to the subsidiary company Ballantine. Because E. N. Ballantine was a nephew of Sykes Cummings, the head editor of Random House, so that's how *This Woman . . . This Woman* was banned in most cities, but in German it was very successful and they called it *Lust Wills Eternity*. Did you ever see a copy of it? I'll show you later—I got it right here. *Lust Wills Eternity*. Years later I finally, only not long ago, completed that dramatization of *This Woman* and it outdoes Pirandello. Someday it's going to be a knockout! It's very long and it runs about four hours. But I spent years working on, slowly and slowly. So that's so much for *This Woman*.

M.D.: *Christ in Concrete*.

P.D.: Well, that's a coincidence, that you're here now. A couple of weeks ago, there was an antique show and a big flea market in the mall, Smithtown [New York]. There was a section there that had back numbers of magazines. So I saw back numbers of *Esquire*. I asked the guy, I said, "I wrote my first short story; it was in 1937." I forgot what month. He said, "Well, I don't have it, but I'll give you the 800 number. There's a big, big outfit in Tucson, Arizona, called 'Chosen Reflections.'" I called him, and sure enough, he had a mint copy of my very first short story. I called him, sent him a check, and it was thirty dollars for the short story, four dollars for the United Parcel and it's due within four or five days—so I'll see that then. Well, I think I told you how I started the short story. I was so emotionalized by the injustice and the iniquity of the Great Depression. Although it was an ill wind that blew me good, because it got me away from bricklaying. Then I was on home relief in Northport. My mother was dead and my sister Anne and I were falling in love with all these kids. I went to the . . . I didn't know what to do with myself. I was unemployed and I went down to the library and I started to read. I read *La Terre*, by Zola. They happened to have classic books there. So when Roosevelt made that speech about the "fear of fears" and so forth, I went and I was so moved, and I said, "He could be; because I was so religious, he could be God's deputy, liberate the masses, continue Jesus' mission." So I wrote him a long letter; he never answered it. Then I wrote him a letter against the Civil War. I wrote a letter to Hitler and I wrote a letter to Mussolini. I called them every Goddamn profane curse word I could think of and they didn't answer. So a Jewish friend of mine, a carpenter, a socialist, he read it. He said, "Jesus Christ"; he said, "You can write." I said, "I can write?" I never wrote a letter. I left school when I was twelve years old. I went to high school three days. But within me the fear that I was going to die like my father, because his father, his foster father—because he was taken out of a foundling home in Abruzzi. That's where I got my name Pietro. He was adopted by a childless couple named Pietro and Theresa Ventura. If his mother hadn't shown up eighteen years later, I would have been Pietro Ventura instead of Pietro DiDonato, because she showed up and proved that she was his mother. But *she* left him at the foundling home. She had been screwed by—of all people—Gabriel D'Annunzio in the mountain village of Taranta Pellinio, where he went there and stayed six months and wrote *La Figlia di Iorio*. I've got the Italian play, probably upstairs, the book from Italy *La Figlia di Iorio*. Pietro Ventura put my father to work when he was seven years old. In Italy they started bricklayers at the age of seven, and my father was a natural, good-looking and strong. While Pietro Ventura was working in on a tunnel and putting in the big shells, the mountain collapsed and crushed him. He was crushed to death. So then my father supported his foster mother, met my mother, got engaged to my mother, when he was twelve and she was twelve. She was also illegitimate. And then when he was eighteen, Geremio, my father, got married. He got summoned by the king to go to Africa in the army, and he wouldn't go. This woman appeared and proved she was his mother and he went to city hall and his name was changed to DiDonato. The mayor showed us; they went to the city 'way back in 1905 or something like that. So he changed his name from Ventura to DiDonato. He came here and he sent for my mother. And they settled in—they were living on Mulberry Street for awhile and then they went across the river to West Hoboken, New Jersey. Then my father was killed. I said, "I'm going to be number three. Before I die, I'm going to move back." I had this need; it was a catharsis. I read at the library. I came across it again—*Fathers and Sons*. And that book inspired me when Bozarro died—Bozarro, the radical nihilist—his father, his gentle father raised his fist against heaven, and he said, "I rebel!" So I said, "I'm going to have my father rebel like I would if this happened to me." And that's how I wrote the short story. Somebody said, "Send this to *Esquire*." Of course that short story becomes the first chapter of the novel, *Christ in Concrete*. I saw a man get killed. I was working on the job, and that turned me, changed me against religion. I realized how my father died; it was a great trauma. I described it in the end of *Christ in Concrete*, when I come home and tell my mother. My mother, of course, smashed my face in, because she would not give up Christ. Christ was the cement that held our lives together. This beautiful, beautiful girl, Stella, a Romanian Jewess American model—I met her in a Communist camp—she was two years older than I. It's a long, long story, but she married, and then she called me during the winter. I met her in the city; she said her husband was going hunting that night, and so forth. And I brought my first short story with a copy and she read it; she read it and left and when he came back from hunting, he came back with horns. I put the horns on him. This was all arranged by her. I never saw such acting in my life. He said, "Send it to *Esquire*; they'll print anything." He's facetious and all that. I did it—bang, they bought it, and then they also made it into, see that small book; they made it into "Christ in Concrete"—a little hard-cover. That's the start, that started it; that's the story.

M.D.: *Three Circles of Light*.

P.D.: I realized that same thing when I wrote *Christ in Concrete*; I never gave a last name to my character. Geremio, Paul, I didn't tell you what it was; that didn't matter, see. You knew it was in the vicinity of New York, so forth and so on. There was so much that had preceded that in the earlier childhood that I felt compelled to . . . it's like I put the cart before the horse. So this way, I was writing a series of little stories, short stories and selling them, so I said, I will put these together from my earliest consciousness. It's only first person; lyricize it and call it *Three Circles of Light*, and it was the face of God in the end of the *Divine Comedy*; if you will recall, she was called Beatrice. He was expecting to see a figure like a man, three rainbows irradiating. So I symbolized each circle—one was the job, one was the home and the other was the church, religion. So it almost made the Book of the Month Club, and the woman who took *Peyton Place*, Kiddie Meisler Publishing House. She loved the material. She edited it. She did a lot of work on it—cut it in half. It was overwritten and she did a beautiful job with it. And when it was done, she said, "It's too good for slobs." And she said, "Why don't you shoot Eisenhower and get some publicity?" In Italy, a lot of Italians, they got more kick out of it than *Christ in Concrete*. But of course *Christ in Concrete* is absolutely pure.

M.D.: "The Gospels."

P.D.: Did you read "Gospels"?

M.D.: Yes, yes.

P.D.: You read "Gospels." I was having a hell of a time trying to get "Gospels" published. They're afraid of it. Fred Gardaphe from Chicago is an editor. He's a hell of a good guy. He's going to publish it in the . . . he bought a quarterly called *Via: Voice of Italian Americans*. Have you seen that? Yes, well, the next issue is going to have quite a few sections of the "Gospels" in it—at present, he feels that somebody in Canada can get it published. It's like . . . when they called me and after my short story was published and said, "Write a couple of chapters on top of this." They didn't give me a contract; they gave me a couple of hundred dollars. When I brought in four chapters they said, "Oh, no; I'm sorry, this will never make a book." They were full of shit, see! Why, Nabokov wrote *Lolita*. No one would publish it, just because your . . . and then with Henry Miller—strange works which are so original that it doesn't fall into the run-of-the-mill slot; the crap they keep publishing, that's what's happening with American writers. You know I think there are more Italians in America than any other race, if I'm not mistaken. That's another thing, but they must reach our phones. But they must reach our phones. You know you don't get the true representation? You've been to Italy? You'd never come back; you'd never come back. Oh, Christ, they're living in the twenty-first century. That's what they tell me last time I was there. You're an American, too. Our people [Italians] are great people.

M.D.: I'll go some day.

P.D.: Well, you stop to think. You've seen our glories on television and all that and so much for Britain or the Roman Empire—so much contributions that they've made to humanity, to society, civilizations. Remember when they degenerated after Caesar? Constantine pulled the switch for him. He took all that Jewish shit, called it Christianity and he made it a compulsory religion. But then he gets away from the Jew element, there, and then they put the Italian people, the Roman and Latin touch to it and—confession and contrition. There was a sensuous rich art like catacombs, music and all that. They centralized it. I never believed in these gods. Why should I believe in the Jew god? But I do love the masses—The Mass. I love the architecture. I love the candles, the incense . . .

Notes

Chapter 1. Introduction

1. Barbara Gae Bauer, introduction to "Cautela, D'Angelo, D'Augustino and DiDonato: The Achievement of First- and Second-Generation Italian-American Writers of the New York Region" (Ph.D. diss., St. John's University of New York, 1979), i.
2. Michael Esposito, "The Travail of Pietro DiDonato," *MELUS* 7, no. 2 (Summer 1980): 47–60.
3. Michael Esposito, "Pietro DiDonato Reevaluated," *Italian-Americana* 6 (Spring/Summer 1980): 182, 189.
4. Giovanni Sinicropi, "Christ in Concrete," *Italian-Americana* 3 (1977): 182 n. 1.
5. Ibid., 188 n. 1.
6. See the works of Carl G. Jung, especially *Modern Man in Search of a Soul* (New York: Harcourt, Brace and World, 1933).

Chapter 2. A Literary Biography

1. Jung, *Modern Man.*
2. Ibid.
3. Bauer, "Cautela," 148.
4. Ibid.

Chapter 3. *The Immigrant Saint: The Life of Mother Cabrini*

1. Esposito, "Travail," 57.
2. Ibid.
3. See Donald W. MacKinnon, "What Makes a Person Creative?" *Saturday Review,* 10 February 1962, 15–17, 69.
4. Jung, *Modern Man.*
5. Nathaniel Hawthorne, *The Scarlet Letter,* in *The Complete Novels and Selected Tales of Nathaniel Hawthorne,* ed. Norman Holmes Pearson (New York: Random House, 1937), 105–6.
6. William F. Lynch, S.J., *Christ and Apollo* (Notre Dame, Ind.: University of Notre Dame Press, 1975), 32.

7. It is intriguing to note how similar Sister Tondini's words are to DiDonato's words about the "strangeness" of life (see Diomede) when she addresses Mother Cabrini: "Somehow we did not get along. I did not mean evil . . . life is strange. And now, why do you stoop to the sight of me, why did you ask for me?" (*IS,* 209).

Chapter 4. *The Penitent*

1. Anthony F. D'Allesandro, "Pietro DiDonato: A Profile," *Italo-American Times,* 24 January 1977, 2, quoted in Esposito, "Travail," 57.
2. Esposito, "Travail," 57.
3. See Fr. Lynch's quotation, which the author has used in discussing DiDonato's other works: "It is not too much to say that the attitude we take toward time, as the most intense form of the limited, on our decision either to strain against or accept it, depends our peace." (*Christ and Apollo,* 32).
4. This phrase, incidentally, was a guiding principle in St. Dominic Savio's life. St. Dominic Savio was a student of St. John Bosco.
5. At times this phrase reminds one of the compassion of Paul's mother, Annunziata, of *Christ in Concrete* and *The Love of Annunziata,* for in these works she is most forgiving of Geremio's [her husband's] sin of betrayal.
6. Dorothy von Huene Greenberg, "A *MELUS* Interview: Pietro DiDonato," *MELUS* 14, nos. 3 and 4 (Fall/Winter 1987): 41.
7. See Jung, *Modern Man,* and his other works.
8. DiDonato tells us that a Cabiniere, returning Alessandro to his hometown after his release from prison, says, "And here I am taking you to freedom and your hometown. The strangeness of life" (131).

Chapter 5. "Christ in Plastic"

1. For another work that exhibits DiDonato's sense of justice, see pages 60–69 and 183–86 of *Christ in Concrete.* Louis Molov, a Russian Jew, a friend of Paul, while they were growing up in the tenement, tells the story of how his family came to America after being persuaded by the Russian czar. Leov, his brother, who protested unfair treatment of the peasants and the war, was killed, like Christ. People in Russia were "starved" (*Christ in Concrete,* 168) and killed (*Christ in Concrete,* 168) by the regime of the czar.
2. Michael Esposito, "A Visionary Speaks: Further Interviews with Pietro DiDonato," *La Parola del Popolo* (Gennaio-Febbraio 1980): 62.
3. Ibid., 61.
4. Ibid., 62.
5. Ibid.
6. Ibid., 62; von Huene-Greenberg, "A *MELUS* Interview, 51.
7. Esposito, "A Visionary Speaks," 62.
8. Ibid.
9. Von Huene-Greenberg, "A *MELUS* Interview," 47.
10. Esposito, "A Visionary Speaks," 62; von Huene-Greenberg, 51.
11. Esposito, "A Visionary Speaks," 62.

12. Ibid., 64.
13. Ibid.
14. Ibid.
15. Von Huene-Greenberg, 44, 52.

Chapter 6. *The Love of Annunziata*

1. For an interesting parallel of forgiveness, see in *The Penitent* how St. Marietta Goretti forgives her murderer, Alessandro Serenelli, and how her own mother, Assunta, also forgives him. The mystery of the love of the Trinity is seen in Goretti's beautiful words to Alessandro, "Christ has forgiven you, and why should not I forgive? I forgive you, of course, my son" (142).

2. For an interesting analogy of the place "home" plays in the redemption of Geremio or Paul, his son, see page 244 in *Three Circles of Light* or my chapter 9 on *Three Circles* in the present volume. In *Three Circles,* Annunziata says that Geremio, after his death, is constructing a "final home" in heaven, but it will not be "complete" until the men and women of the family have children of their own, until they "ceaselessly pray" (244). I do not think the home is "complete" until Paul really develops most fully in *This Woman,* as I try to show later. *This Woman,* in my opinion, is DiDonato's best novel.

3. Annunziata's denial is accentuated in greater detail and with more emotion in her dance at the funeral scene in *Three Circles,* though she still accepts Geremio in that work. The dichotomy of Annunziata's love and hate for Geremio appears to be more marked in *Three Circles* than in *The Love of Annunziata*.

4. For an interesting parallel of how we must all slay the "dragon" in us, that which deters us from fully developing as humans, see Erich Neumann, *The Origins and History of Consciousness* (Princeton: Princeton University Press, 1954): 199, and esp. pt. 1, sec. B. A rather intriguing book that makes the point that we must "die" to that within us that can "slay" us is Maud Bodkin's *Archetypal Patterns in Poetry* (New York: Oxford University Press, 1934), 34.

5. See Bauer, "Cautela," 148 for a penetrating analysis of Annunziata.

6. Rose Basile Green, *The Italian American Novel* (Rutherford, N.J.: Fairleigh Dickinson University Press, 1974), 147; Bauer, "Cautela," 147–48.

7. Bauer, "Cautela," 129–30.
8. Ibid., 157.
9. Ibid., 155.
10. See Lynch, *Christ and Apollo.*

Chapter 7. *This Woman*

1. Bauer, "Cautela," 143.
2. Green, *Italian American Novel,* 155, 165.
3. Ibid., 155.
4. Esposito, "Travail," 56.
5. For more on this theme of dying or slaying the "dragon" that holds us back from developing into maturity, see Maud Bodkin, *Archetypal Patterns*; Martin Buber,

I and Thou (New York: Charles Scribner's Sons, 1958); Joseph Campbell, *The Hero with a Thousand Faces,* 2d ed., Bollingen ser. 17 (Princeton: Princeton University Press, 1958); Lynch, *Christ and Apollo;* Jung, *Modern Man;* Erich Neumann, *The Origins and History of Consciousness;* Walter J. Ong, S.J., *Fighting for Life: Contest, Sexuality, and Consciousness* (Ithaca: Cornell University Press, 1981); Victor White, O.P., *God and the Unconscious* (Cleveland: World Publishing, 1952); Victor Frankl, *Man's Search for Meaning: An Introduction to Logotherapy* (Boston: Beacon Press, 1962).

6. Pietro DiDonato quoted in Matthew Diomede, "A Personal Interview with Pietro DiDonato, Held August 14, 1990," chap. 2 in "Pietro DiDonato, The Master Builder: Constructing a Better World with Concrete and Love, A Study of Selected Works and of the Author" (Ph.D. diss., St. Louis University, 1992); see app. A in the present volume.

7. Bauer, "Cautela," 143.

8. Green, *Italian American Novel,* 143, 155, 165.

9. It is interesting to note that in *Three Circles* when Geremio asks pregnant Annunziata to go to the theater, Annunziata, after scolding Geremio for being too tired to go to mass, makes an interesting contrast between church and the theater: "Better my baby is born before Holy Altar than in clowning temple of faked emotions" *(Three Circles of Light,* 206). (The temple is the theater referred to in the previous paragraph of the novel wherein Geremio and Paul's "godmother," Delia Dunn [Diane Dunn in *This Woman*] sang and danced as a team. Delia bears Geremio's son out of wedlock; see chap. 21 of *Three Circles of Light.*)

10. Esposito, "Travail," 56.

11. Von Huene-Greenberg, "A *MELUS* Interview," 47.

12. Ibid.

13. Ibid.

14. See the books of Yeats, Lynch, Campbell, and Neumann.

15. See Father Walter J. Ong, *Fighting for Life: Contest, Sexuality, and Consciousness* for an explanation of male and female components, esp. pp. 99–103. See also the works of Carl G. Jung.

Chapter 8. *Christ in Concrete*

1. Harry M. Geduld, "*Christ in Concrete:* Fiction in Film," *Rivista di Studi Anglo-America* 3, nos. 4 and 5 (1984–85): 252.

2. Ibid.

3. Warren French, *The Social Novel at the End of an Era* (Carbondale: Southern Illinois University Press, 1966), 182.

4. Nathaniel Hawthorne, preface to *The House of Seven Gables,* in *Complete Novels and Plays,* 243, quoted in Richard Chase, *The American Novel and Its Tradition* (Baltimore: Johns Hopkins University Press, 1957), 20.

5. Chase, *American Novel,* 49.

6. William Faulkner, "Nobel Prize Acceptance Speech," in *From Thought to Theme,* ed. William F. Smith and Raymond D. Liedlich (New York: Harcourt, Brace and World, 1964), 393.

7. Chase, *American Novel,* 20.

8. Faulkner, "Nobel Speech," 393.
9. Ibid., 393.
10. Chase, *American Novel*, 19.
11. Faulkner, "Nobel Speech," 393.
12. Michael Esposito, "Pietro DiDonato: Forty Years After," *La Parola del Popola* (November/December 1979): 65; idem, "Travail," 47; idem, "Pietro DiDonato Reevaluated," 182.
13. Nicholas Coles, "Mantraps: Men at Work, in Pietro DiDonato's *Christ in Concrete* and Thomas Bell's 'Out of This Furnace,'" *MELUS* 14, nos. 3 and 4 (Fall/Winter 1987): 26; Bauer, "Cautela," 125, 126.
14. For an interesting analysis of the use of the concept of the Incarnation in literature and in psychology, see Raymond Benoit, *Single Nature's Double Meaning* (The Hague: Mouton, 1973).
15. See Lynch, *Christ and Apollo*.
16. See ibid. and Benoit, *Single Nature's Double Meaning*.
17. Gen. 3, in *The New Living Bible* (Wheaton, Ill.: Tyndale House, 1971).
18. Von Huene-Greenberg, "A *MELUS* Interview," 36.
19. Halford Luccock feels in *American Mirror: Social, Ethical and Religious Aspects of American Literature, 1930–40* (New York: Macmillan, 1940), 146, 174, that DiDonato can be classified as a writer of proletarian literature of the 1930s.
20. Esposito, "Pietro DiDonato Reevaluated," 179, 191; idem, "A Visionary Speaks," 63, 65.
21. von Huene-Greenberg, "A *MELUS* Interview," 35; Esposito, "Pietro DiDonato Reevaluated," 179.
22. Esposito, "Travail," 55.
23. Von Huene-Greenberg, "A *MELUS* Interview," 40.
24. Geduld, "*Christ in Concrete*," 235.
25. Nathaniel Hawthorne, preface to *The House of Seven Gables*, 243, quoted in Chase, *American Novel*, 20.
26. Faulkner, "Nobel Speech," 393.
27. Henry James, *The Ambassadors* (London: Penguin, 1986), 215.
28. This passage parallels a most vital passage of DiDonato's literature, the ending of *This Woman* where Paul plays with his child and in the presence of his wife. The beach scene is representative of "home" and the "heart"—Paul becomes father of a family in *This Woman* (217, 220).
29. This is another vital passage. I feel Paul's "Catholic Soul" at the end of *This Woman* (220) saves him and his family. This passage in *This Woman* is the culmination of DiDonato's literature and is representative of the fact that Paul has become a man.
30. Von Huene-Greenberg, "A *MELUS* Interview," 38.
31. See Carl Jung's books, especially *Modern Man in Search of a Soul*.
32. See similar books exploring the theme of the quest to find a home: Homer, *The Odyssey of Homer* (New York: Henry Z. Walck, 1952); William Saroyan, *The Human Comedy* (New York: Harcourt, Brace and World, 1943). It is interesting to note that *The Human Comedy* stressed the return to home in the midst of the war experience. Incidentally, Mr. Saroyan appears as an Armenian coffee-and-nut store owner in *Three Circles of Light*, 11.
33. See Jung, especially *Modern Man in Search of a Soul*.

34. See Lynch, *Christ and Apollo;* Jung, *Modern Man;* and Benoit, *Single Nature's Double Meaning.*
35. Bauer, "Cautela," 148.
36. Ibid.
37. Hawthorne, preface to *The House of Seven Gables,* 243, quoted in Chase, *American Novel,* 20.
38. Faulkner, "Nobel Speech," 393; French, *Social Novel,* 181–82.
39. See Lynch, *Christ and Apollo;* Campbell, *Hero;* and Neumann, *Origins and History.*

Chapter 9. *Three Circles of Light*

1. For an interesting discussion of the concept of the expiation of sins in Geremio's and Paul's lives, see Bauer, "Cautela," 145–49, 162. I do not agree with Bauer, however, that *Three Circles of Light* is perhaps DiDonato's best novel, as I try to show in chap. 7 in the present volume.

Chapter 10. Conclusion

1. See Lynch, *Christ and Apollo.*
2. See Campbell, *The Hero;* Jung, *Modern Man;* and Neumann, *Origins and History.*
3. See Campbell, *The Hero;* Jung, *Modern Man;* and Neumann, *Origins and History.*
4. Suzanne K. Langer, *Problems of Art,* 71.

Appendix B. Personal Interview, 8 August 1991

1. See Pietro DiDonato's article, "My People, My Place," *Coronet* 44 (September 1958): 34–45.

Bibliography

Primary Works

FICTION

DiDonato, Pietro. *Christ in Concrete.* Indianapolis: Bobbs-Merrill, 1939.
———. "The Gospels." Unpublished.
———. *This Woman.* New York: Ballantine, 1959.
———. *Three Circles of Light.* New York: Julian Messner, 1960.

NONFICTION

———. "Christ in Plastic." *Penthouse,* December 1978, 3, 76, 78, 80, 82, 222–24, 226, 229–31.
———. *The Immigrant Saint: The Life of Mother Cabrini.* New York: McGraw-Hill, 1960.
———. "My People, My Place." *Coronet* 44 (September 1958): 34–45.
———. *The Penitent.* New York: Hawthorne, 1962.

DRAMA

———. *The Love of Annunziata.* In *American Scenes,* edited by William Kozlenko, 119–38. New York: McGraw-Hill, 1941.

Secondary Works

Adamic, Louis. "Muscular Novel of Immigrant Life." *Saturday Review of Literature* 26 August 1969, 5.
Backman, Melvin. *Faulkner: The Major Years.* Bloomington: Indiana University Press, 1966.
Barbato, Joseph. "Once Upon a Time I Created a Classic." *National Observer,* 20 March 1976, 32.

Bauer, Barbara Gae. "Cautela, D'Angelo, D'Augustino and DiDonato: The Achievement of First- and Second-Generation Italian-American Writers of the New York Region." Ph.D. diss., St. John's University of New York, 1979.

Benoit, Raymond. *Single Nature's Double Meaning*. The Hague: Mouton, 1973.

Bodkin, Maud. *Archetypal Patterns in Poetry*. New York: Oxford University Press, 1934.

Boelhower, William. "Ethnic Trilogies: A Genealogical and Generational Poetics." In *The Invention of Ethnicity,* edited by Werner Sollors, 158–75. New York: Oxford University Press, 1989.

———. "The Ethnic Trilogy: A Poetics of Cultural Passage." *MELUS* 12, no. 4 (Winter 1985): 7–23.

———. *Immigrant Autobiography in the U.S.*. Verona: Essedue, Edizione, 1982.

———. "The Immigrant Novel as Genre." *MELUS* 8, no. 1 (Spring 1981): 3–14.

———. *Through a Glass Darkly Ethnic Semiosis in American Literature*. New York: Oxford University Press, 1987.

Buber, Martin. *I and Thou*. New York: Charles Scribner's Sons, 1958.

Cammett, John M., ed. *The Italian-American Novel: Proceedings of the Second Annual Conference*, 25 October 1969. Staten Island, N. Y.: The American-Italian Historical Association, n.d.

Campbell, Joseph. *The Hero With a Thousand Faces*. 2d ed. Bollingen ser. 15. Princeton: Princeton University Press, 1958.

Canfield, Dorothy. "A Young Bricklayer Writes." Review of *Christ in Concrete,* by Pietro DiDonato. *New York Times Book Review*, 20 August 1939, 28.

Casciato, Arthur D. "The Bricklayer as Bricoleur: Pietro DiDonato and the Cultural Politics of the Popular Front." *VIA: Voices in Italian Americana* 2, no. 2 (Fall 1991): 67–78.

Chase, Richard. *The American Novel and Its Tradition*. Baltimore: Johns Hopkins University Press, 1957.

Coles, Nicholas. "Mantraps: Men at Work, in Pietro DiDonato's *Christ in Concrete* and Thomas Bell's 'Out of This Furnace.'" *MELUS* 14, nos. 3 and 4 (Fall-Winter 1987): 23–32.

Cordasco, Francesco. *Italians in the United States: A Bibliography*. New York: Oriole, 1972.

D'Allesandro, F. Anthony. "Pietro DiDonato: A Profile." *Italo-American Times*, 24 January 1977, 2.

Davidson, Carter. "The Immigrant Strain in Contemporary American Literature." *English Journal* 25 (1936): 862–68.

Davis, Rebecca Harding. *Life in the Iron Mills*. Introduction by Tillie Olsen. New York: Feminist Press, 1972.

Dickens, Charles. *A Tale of Two Cities*. New York: Houghton Mifflin, 1962.

Dostoyevsky, Fyodor. *Crime and Punishment*. New York: Modern Library, 1950.

Esposito, Michael. "Pietro DiDonato: Forty Years After." *La Parola del Popolo* Novembre-Dicembre 1979, 65–67.

———. "Pietro DiDonato Reevaluated." *Italian-Americana* 6 (Spring-Summer 1980): 179–92.

———. "The Travail of Pietro DiDonato." *MELUS* 7, no. 2 (Summer 1980): 47–60.

———. "A Visionary Speaks: Further Interviews with Pietro DiDonato." *La Parola del Popolo,* Gennaio-Febbraio 1980, 61–64.

Faulkner, William. *As I Lay Dying.* New York: Vintage, 1964.

———. "Nobel Prize Acceptance Speech." In *From Thought to Theme,* edited by William F. Smith and Raymond D. Liedlich, 392–93. New York: Harcourt, Brace and World, 1965.

Feifel, Herman. *The Meaning of Death.* New York: McGraw-Hill, 1965.

Ferraro, Thomas J. "Ethnicity and the Marketplace." In vol. 1 of *The Columbia History of the American Novel,* edited by Emory Elliot. New York: Columbia University Press, 1991.

Frankl, Victor. *Man's Search for Meaning: An Introduction to Logotherapy.* Boston: Beacon, 1962.

French, Warren. *The Social Novel at the End of an Era.* Carbondale: Southern Illinois University Press, 1966.

Freud, Sigmund. *Civilization and Its Discontents.* New York: W. W. Norton, 1961.

Friend, Joseph H. Review of *Christ in Concrete,* by Pietro DiDonato. *New York Herald Tribune,* 20 August 1939, 4.

Gardaphe, Fred L. "From Oral Tradition to Written Word: Toward an Ethnographically Based Literary Criticism." In *From the Margin: Writings in Italian Americana,* edited by Anthony Julian Tamburri, Paolo A. Giordano, and Fred L. Gardaphe, 294-306. West Lafayette, Ind.: Purdue University Press, 1991.

———. Introduction to *Christ in Concrete,* by Pietro DiDonato. New York: New American Library, 1993.

———. "Italian-American Fiction: A Third-Generation Renaissance." *MELUS* 14, nos. 3 and 4 (Fall-Winter 1987): 69–85.

Garside, E. B. Review of *Christ in Concrete,* by Pietro DiDonato. *Atlantic Monthly,* September 1939.

Geduld, Harry M. "*Christ in Concrete*: Fiction in Film." *Rivista di Studi Anglo-America* 3, nos. 4 and 5 (1984–85): 241–56.

Giles, Paul. *American Catholic Arts and Fictions Culture, Ideology, Aesthetics.* New York: Cambridge University Press, 1992.

Gingrich, Arnold. "A Terrific Fuss Over a Story." *Esquire,* March 1937, 5, 32.

Giordano, Paolo A. "From Southern Italian Emigrant to Reluctant American: Joseph Tusiani's *Gente Mia and Other Poems.*" In *From the Margin: Writings in Italian Americana,* edited by Anthony Julian Tamburri, Paolo A. Giordano, and Fred L. Gardaphe, 316–28. West Lafayette, Ind.: Purdue University Press, 1991.

Glazer, Nathan, and Daniel Patrick Moynihan. *Beyond the Melting Pot: The Negroes, Puerto Ricans, Jews, Italians, and Irish of New York City.* Cambridge: MIT Press, 1963.

Green, Rose Basile. "The Evolution of Italian-American Fiction As a Document of the Interaction of Two Cultures." Ph.D. diss., University of Pennsylvania, 1962.

———. *The Italian-American Novel.* Rutherford, N.J.: Fairleigh Dickinson University Press, 1974.

Hawthorne, Nathaniel. Preface to *The House of Seven Gables.* In *The Complete Novels and Selected Tales of Nathaniel Hawthorne,* edited by Norman Holmes Pearson, 242–43. New York: Random House.

———. *The Scarlet Letter.* In *The Complete Novels and Selected Tales of Nathaniel Hawthorne,* edited by Norman Holmes Pearson, 85–240. New York: Random House, 1937.

Heal, Edith, ed. *I Wanted to Write a Poem: The Autobiography of the Works of a Poet,* by William Carlos Williams. Boston: Beacon, 1958.

Homer. *The Odyssey of Homer.* New York: Henry Z. Walck, 1952.

James, Henry. *The Ambassadors.* London: Penguin, 1986.

Johnson, Tom. "Pietro DiDonato, *il professore dei trovator,*" *VIA: Voices in Italian Americana* 2, no. 2 (Fall 1991): 51–58.

Jung, Carl G. *Man and His Symbols.* New York: Dell, 1964.

———. *Modern Man in Search of a Soul.* New York: Harcourt, Brace and World, 1933.

———. *Psyche and Symbol.* New York: Doubleday, 1958.

———. *Memories, Dreams, Reflections.* Edited by Aniela Jaffe. New York: Vintage, 1963.

Kunitz, Stanley, ed. *Twentieth-Century Authors.* New York: H. W. Wilson, 1955.

Langer, Suzanne K. *Problems of Art.* New York: Scribner's, 1957.

Luccock, Halford F. *American Mirror: Social, Ethical, and Religious Aspects of American Literature, 1930–1940.* New York: Macmillan, 1940.

Lynch, William F., S. J. *Christ and Apollo.* Notre Dame, Ind.: University of Notre Dame Press, 1975.

MacKinnon, Donald W. "What Makes a Person Creative?" *Saturday Review,* 10 February 1962, 15–17, 69.

Mangione, Anthony Ray. "The Story That Has Not Been Told: A Selective Bibliography Dealing with the Italian-American Experience." *English Record,* Winter 1973–74, 25–34.

Mangione, Jerre. Review of *Christ in Concrete,* by Pietro DiDonato. *New York Times Book Review,* 20 August 1939, 6.

Marsh, Fred T. Review of *Christ in Concrete,* by Pietro DiDonato. *New York Times Book Review,* 20 August 1939, 6.

Melpezzi, Frances M., and William M. Clements. *Italian-American Folklore.* Little Rock, Ark.: August House, 1992.

Meyer, Adam. "The Need for Cross-Ethnic Studies: A Manifesto (with Antipasto)." *MELUS* 16, no. 4 (Winter 1989–90): 19–39.

Mulas, Franco. "The Ethnic Language of Pietro DiDonato's *Christ in Concrete.*" In *From the Margin: Writings in Italian Americana,* edited by Anthony Julian Tamburri, Paolo A. Giordano, and Fred L. Gardaphe, 307-15. West Lafayette, Ind.: Purdue University Press, 1991.

———. "A MELUS Interview: Jerre Mangione." *MELUS* 12, no. 4 (Winter 1985): 73–87.

Neumann, Erich. *The Origins and History of Consciousness.* Princeton: Princeton University Press, 1954.

Ong, Walter J., S. J. *Fighting for Life: Contest, Sexuality and Consciousness.* Ithaca: Cornell University Press, 1981.

Palmer, Patricia. Review of *Christ in Concrete,* by Pietro DiDonato. *Canadian Forum* 19, no. 225 (December 1939): 294–95.

Patti, Samuel J. "Recent Italian American Literature: The Case of John Fante." In *From the Margin: Writings in Italian Americana,* edited by Anthony Julian Tamburri, Paolo A. Giordano, and Fred L. Gardaphe, 329-37. West Lafayette, Ind.: Purdue University Press, 1991.

Peragallo, O. *Italian-American Authors and Their Contribution to American Literature.* New York: S. F. Vanni, 1949.

Poore, G. Review of *Christ in Concrete,* by Pietro DiDonato. *New York Times* 15 September 1939, 27.

Review of *Christ in Concrete. Christian Century* 56 (4 October 1939): 1203–4.

Review of *Christ in Concrete. Times Literary Supplement,* 21 October 1931, 611.

Review of *Christ in Concrete. Manchester Guardian,* 17 October 1931, 3.

Review of *Christ in Concrete. New Statesman and Nation* 18 (21 October 1939): 57.

Review of *Christ in Concrete. New Yorker,* 2 September 1939, 57.

Review of *Christ in Concrete. Pratt,* Winter 1940, 23.

Review of *Christ in Concrete. Publishers Weekly,* 19 August 1939, 534.

Review of *Christ in Concrete. Time,* 10 April 1939, 75, 77.

Review of *Three Circles of Light. Booklist* 56, no. 20 (1960): 626.

Review of *Three Circles of Light. Commonweal* 72 (1960): 429.

Review of *Three Circles of Light. Kirkus* 28 (1960): 251.

Review of *Three Circles of Light. Library Journal* 85, no. 7 (1960): 1472.

Review of *Three Circles of Light. San Francisco Chronicle*, 7 August 1960, 18.

Review of *Three Circles of Light. Time,* 6 June 1960, 101.

Rideout, Walter. *The Radical Novel in the United States.* New York: Hill and Wang, 1956.

Rodriguez, Richard. "An American Writer." In *The Invention of Ethnicity,* edited by Werner Sollors, 3-13. New York: Oxford University Press, 1989.

Russo, John Paul. "The Choice of Gilbert Sorrentino." In *From the Margin: Writings in Italian Americana,* edited by Anthony Julian Tamburri, Paolo A. Giordano, and Fred L. Gardaphe, 338-56. West Lafayette, Ind.: Purdue University Press, 1991.

Salinger, J. D. *The Catcher in the Rye.* New York: Bantam, 1951.

Salomon, Louis B. Review of *Christ in Concrete,* by Pietro DiDonato. *Nation* 49, no. 9 (1939): 223.

Salvatori, Mariolina. "Women's Work in Novels of Immigrant Life." *MELUS* 9, no. 4 (Winter 1982): 39–58.

Saroyan, William. *The Human Comedy*. New York: Harcourt, Brace and World, 1943.

Sinclair, Upton. *The Jungle*. New York: New American Library, 1960.

Sinicropi, Giovanni. "Christ in Concrete." *Italian Americana* 3 (1977): 175–83.

Sollors, Werner. *Beyond Ethnicity: Consent and Descent in American Culture*. New York: Oxford University Press, 1986.

———, ed. *The Invention of Ethnicity*. New York: Oxford University Press, 1989.

Stevenson, Robert Louis. "Markheim." In *Fiction 100*, 1st ed., 890–99. New York: Macmillan, 1974.

Tamburri, Anthony Julian, Paolo A. Giordano, and Fred L. Gardaphe, eds. *From the Margin: Writings in Italian Americana*. West Lafayette, Ind.: Purdue University Press, 1991.

Thompson, Ralph. Review of *Christ in Concrete*, by Pietro DiDonato. *Yale Review* 29, no. 1 (September 1939): vi, viii.

Von Huene-Greenberg, Dorothee. "A *MELUS* Interview: Pietro DiDonato." *MELUS* 14, nos. 3 and 4 (Fall-Winter 1987): 33–52.

Walsh, Chad. Review of *Three Circles of Light*, by Pietro DiDonato. *New York Herald Tribune*, 5 June 1960, 8.

White, Victor, O. P. *God and the Unconscious*. Cleveland: World Publishing, 1952.

Yeats, William Butler. *The Collected Poems of W. B. Yeats*. New York: Macmillan, 1977.

Index

Abruzzi, Italy, 17, 79, 80, 109, 134, 145
Ambassadors, The (James), 79
American Italian Historical Association, 109, 122
American Novel and Its Tradition, The (Chase), 151n. 4
Arnold, Eve, 116, 132
As I Lay Dying (Faulkner), 62
Awake and Sing (Odets), 111

Ballantine, E. N., 9, 119, 143, 144
Bari, Italy, 109
Bauer, Barbara Gae, 15, 54, 56, 68, 71, 129, 148n. 1, 150n. 5, 153n. 1
Beatrice (*Paradiso, The Divine Comedy*), 131, 146
Benoit, Raymond, 11, 152nn. 14 and 16, 153n. 34
Bobbs-Merrill, 9, 112
Bodkin, Maud, 98, 150nn. 4 and 5
Buber, Martin, 150n. 5

Campbell, Joseph, 150n. 5, 153nn. 3, 4, and 39
"Canto 33" (*Paradiso, Divine Comedy*), 92, 131
Catcher in the Rye, The (Salinger), 89
Cerf, Bennett, 118, 119, 144
Chase, Richard, 72, 151nn. 5 and 7, 152n. 10, 153n. 37
Christ and Apollo (Lynch), 148
Christian Democrats, 41, 45, 141
Coles, Nicholas, 152n. 13
Cooperstown, New York, 103, 136, 143, 144
Coronet, 132, 133, 153n. 1
Crime and Punishment (*Delitto e Pena*, Dostoevsky), 53, 64, 141
Cummings, Sykes, 118, 144
Cuomo, Mario, 106, 117, 126

D'Alessandro, Anthony F., 128, 149n. 1
Dante Alighieri, 37, 44, 92, 105, 131
Davis, Rebecca Harding, 82
Death of a Salesman (Miller), 60
Democratic Vistas (Whitman), 111
Dickens, Charles, 75
DiDonato, Pietro: his conceptual statements, beliefs, ideas, 19–21; love/death, 105; love/God/beauty/his wife/woman, 100, 143; loving good and beautiful people, 100–101, 105, 113–14; philosophy of writing, 104; protest/rebellion, 101; sacredness/mystery of life, 104–5, 113–14; value of dreams, 102–3. *Works* (abbreviations notated in the text follow names of works): *Christ in Concrete* (CC), 71–88; "Christ in Plastic" (CIP), 41–46; "The Gospels" (TG), 9, 42, 105, 106, 107, 129, 138, 146, 147; *The Immigrant Saint: The Life of Mother Cabrini* (IS), 23–30; *The Love of Annunziata* (LOA), 47–55; *The Penitent* (TP), 31–40; *This Woman* (TW), 56–70; *Three Circles of Light* (TCOL), 89–96; *Venus Odyssey*, 100
Dostoevsky, Fyodor, 32, 37, 63, 127, 130, 141

Dmytryk, Edward, 71, 121

Easter, 47, 48, 49, 51, 141
Esposito, Michael, 15, 41, 42, 44, 56, 69, 71, 128, 129, 136, 137
Esquire, 41, 73, 112, 144, 146, 147
Ethnic literature, 108

Fathers and Sons (Turgenev), 147
Faulkner, William, 57, 62, 72, 79, 152n. 6
Fellini, Federico, 121, 122
Francis of Assisi, Saint, 80
French, Warren, 72, 151n. 3, 153n. 38
Freud, Sigmund, 83

Gardaphe, Fred, 147, 160
Geduld, Harry M., 71, 72
Good Friday, 47, 48, 49, 50, 51, 73, 82, 91, 93, 112, 117, 141
Grapes of Wrath, The (Steinbeck), 103
Green, Rose Basile, 15, 54, 56, 68, 71
Grierton, Father, 116, 140

Hawthorne, Nathaniel, 25, 72, 77, 110, 148n. 5, 151n. 4, 152n. 25, 153n. 37
Heal, Edith, 16, 138
Hemingway, Ernest, 43, 111, 142
Hitler, Adolf, 113, 126, 145
Homer, 152n. 32
Human Comedy, The (Saroyan), 132, 153n. 32

I Wanted to Write a Poem (Heal), 16, 138

James, Henry, 55, 79, 152n. 27
Jesuits, 27
Jung, Carl, 17, 21, 24, 31, 39, 46, 84, 98, 148, 149, 151, 153
Jungle, The (Sinclair), 82

Kozlenko, William, 9, 142

La Terre (Zola), 145
Langer, Suzanne K., 98, 153n. 4
Lewis, Sinclair, 118

Life in the Iron Mills (Davis), 82
Lolita (Nabokov), 147
Lombardi, John, 41, 42, 142
Loren Sophia, 113, 139
Luccock, Halford, 152n. 19
Lynch, William F., S.J., 30, 98, 149n. 3

MacKinnon, Donald W., 23, 100, 148n. 3
Mailer, Norman, 119
Manzoni, Alessandro
"Markheim" (Stevenson), 32, 63
Mauro, Father, 114, 140
McGraw-Hill, 9, 101, 139
MELUS, 99
Miller, Arthur, 60, 110
Miller, Henry, 147
Modern City (This Woman), 59, 136
Modern Man in Search of a Soul (Jung), 31, 148nn. 1, 4, and 6, 149n. 7, 152n. 31
Molov, Louis, 75, 76, 149n. 1
Montesi, Dr. Al F., 11, 116, 122
Moro, Aldo, 21, 22, 41, 42, 43, 44, 45, 46, 138, 141
Mussolini, Benito, 145
My Lai, Vietnam, 99

Nabokov, Vladimir, 147
Nazone, Vincenzo *(Christ in Concrete),* 73, 79, 80, 81, 82, 88, 134
New Adam, 17, 18, 19, 69, 86, 94, 97, 98
Northport Journal, 111

Odets, Clifford, 111
Odyssey, The (Homer), 132, 152n. 32
O'Hara, John, 118
Old Adam, 17, 18, 61, 69, 86, 94, 95, 96, 97
O'Neill, Eugene, 118
Ong, Walter J., S.J., 9, 151n. 15
Orwell, George, 101

Paesanos, 52, 54, 55, 78, 111
Pellegrini, Angelo, 109
Penthouse, 9, 41, 141
Piazzo Diomede, 107

Pirandello, Luigi, 127, 144
Playboy, 100, 142
Promised Bride, The (Manzoni), 37

Red Brigade (BR, RB, Brigate Rosse), 41, 42, 43, 44, 45, 46, 141, 142
Resurrection, 48, 49, 51, 141
Raskolnikov *(Crime and Punishment),* 33, 37, 63
Rossellini, Roberto, 121
Rossi, Franco, 121

Salinger, J. D., 89
San Christobel, 142
Saroyan, William, 132, 152n. 32
Scala Santa, 114, 140
Schwartz, Delmore, 130
Sinclair, Upton, 82
Sinicropi, Giovanni, 15, 148n. 4
Six Characters in Search of an Author (Pirandello), 127
Skokie, Illinois, 108
Skouras, George, 139
Smithtown, New York, 143, 144
Stevenson, Robert Louis, 32, 63
St. Louis University, 10, 116, 151n. 6
Stone, I. F., 112

Stony Brook University, 106
Strether, Lambert *(The Ambassadors),* 79

Tale of Two Cities, A (Dickens), 75
Tarantella, 20, 47, 48, 52, 54, 85, 92
Tondini, Sister Antonio *(The Immigrant Saint),* 25, 29, 30, 149n. 7
Twentieth Century Fox, 113, 139

Utica, New York, 136

Van Winkle, Rip, 37
Vasto, Italy, 107, 108, 134
Villon, Francis, 107
Von Huene Greenberg, Dorothy, 37, 69, 74, 86, 99

West Hoboken, New Jersey, 31, 91, 110, 114, 139, 146
White, Victor, O.P., 150n. 5
Whitman, Walt, 111
Williams, William Carlos, 16, 138

Yeats, William Butler, 151n. 14
Zola, Emile, 145